**Negrophobia and Reasonable Racism**

## Critical America

### General Editors: RICHARD DELGADO and JEAN STEFANCIC

*White by Law: The Legal Construction of Race*
Ian F. Haney López

*Cultivating Intelligence: Power, Law, and the Politics of Teaching*
Louise Harmon and Deborah W. Post

*Privilege Revealed: How Invisible Preference Undermines America*
Stephanie M. Wildman with Margalynne Armstrong,
Adrienne D. Davis, and Trina Grillo

*Does the Law Morally Bind the Poor? or What Good's the
Constitution When You Can't Afford a Loaf of Bread*
R. George Wright

*Hybrid: Bisexuals, Multiracials, and Other Misfits under American Law*
Ruth Colker

*Critical Race Feminism: A Reader*
Edited by Adrien Katherine Wing

*Immigrants Out! The New Nativism and the Anti-Immigrant
Impulse in the United States*
Edited by Juan F. Perea

*Taxing America*
Edited by Karen B. Brown and Mary Louise Fellows

*Notes of a Racial Caste Baby: Colorblindness and the End of
Affirmative Action*
Bryan K. Fair

*Please Don't Wish Me a Merry Christmas:
A Critical History of the Separation of Church and State*
Stephen M. Feldman

*To Be an American: Cultural Pluralism and the
Rhetoric of Assimilation*
Bill Ong Hing

*Negrophobia and Reasonable Racism: The Hidden Costs of
Being Black in America*
Jody David Armour

*Black Rage Confronts the Law*
Paul Harris

# NEGROPHOBIA

## AND REASONABLE RACISM

The Hidden Costs of Being Black in America

Jody David Armour

NEW YORK UNIVERSITY PRESS

New York and London

**NEW YORK UNIVERSITY PRESS**
New York and London

Library of Congress Cataloging-in-Publication Data
Armour, Jody David.
Negrophobia and reasonable racism : the hidden costs of being
Black in America / Jody David Armour.
p. cm. — (Critical America)
Includes bibliographical references (p. ) and index.
ISBN 0-8147-0640-1 (acid-free paper)
1. Discrimination in criminal justice administration—United States.
2. Afro-Americans—Civil rights. 3. Racism—United States.
4. United States—Race relations. I. Title. II. Series.
HV9950.A75 1997
305.896′073—dc21      96-51306
CIP

New York University Press books are printed on acid-free paper,
and their binding materials are chosen for strength and durability.

Manufactured in the United States of America
10  9  8  7  6  5  4  3  2  1

To Addie Armour
and in memory of
Fred Armour

# CONTENTS

*Acknowledgments*  *ix*

**Introduction**

"Rational" Discrimination and the Black Tax  1

**Chapter One**

The "Reasonable Racist": A Slippery Oxymoron  19

How We Know What We Know: The Typical,
the Reasonable, and the Accurate  22

Why We Blame Whom We Blame: The Typical,
the Reasonable, and the Damnable  27

**Chapter Two**

The "Intelligent Bayesian":
Reckoning with Rational Discrimination  35

Why Rational Discrimination Is Not Reasonable  46

Race and the Subversion of Rationality  58

**Chapter Three**

The "Involuntary Negrophobe"   61

The Involuntary Negrophobe and Dueling Conceptions of Law   64

**Chapter Four**

Of Mice and Men: Equal Protection and Unconscious Bias   68

Private Bias and Equal Protection   69

Restructuring the Maze to Serve Justice   77

**Chapter Five**

Blame and Punishment: Narrative, Perspective, Scapegoats,
and Demons   81

Framing the Narrative Broadly in Women's Self-Defense Work   83

Narrative, Consent, and Blame   84

The Fundamental Fault Line: Determinism
versus Antideterminism   89

"Disadvantaged Social Background"   94

Opponents Grasp at Straws   96

Ideological Agendas   101

**Chapter Six**

Repealing the Black Tax: Breaking the
Discrimination Habit   115

Hypocritical Racists and Aversive Racists   118

Proving Ubiquitous Unconscious Bias   130

Combating Unconscious Discrimination in the Courtroom   139

**Conclusion**   154

*Notes*   161

*Index*   201

# ACKNOWLEDGMENTS

I presented portions of this book at various workshops, colloquia, and faculty seminars in Colorado, Indiana, Pittsburgh, and
at the University of Southern California. I gained much from
these workshops, seminars, and colloquia, and thank all those
who participated. Parts of the book were also presented at the
American Association on Law Schools Conference on Torts and
at another AALS Conference on Evidence. I received valuable
comments from participants at both conferences.

Outside these organized forums, Phreda Devereaux provided
extremely helpful remarks on the chapter on Negrophobia;
Frank McClelland offered penetrating comments on the chapter
on stereotypes and prejudice; and Martha Chamallas, Jules
Lobel, Rhonda Wasserman, and Welsh White read large portions of the manuscript, making many very thoughtful remarks.

The discussions of battered women benefited greatly from suggestions by Veronica Hobbs of Advocates for Basic Legal Equality. I am also indebted to Martine Beauman, Rhonda Evans, Dominck Lee, Piyush Seth, and Christopher White for valuable research assistance, and to LuAnn Driscoll, Karen Knochel, Darleen Mocello, Carolyn Rohan, and Barbara Salopek for patient, precise, tireless document processing assistance.

I am also grateful to my editors, Richard Delgado, Niko Pfund, and Jean Stefancic, and to New York University Press. And I am thankful to the following journals for permission to use portions of essays that first appeared in their pages: Stanford Law Review, Race Ipsa Loquitur: Of Reasonable Racists, Intelligent Bayesians, and Involuntary Negrophobes [46 Stan. L. Rev. 781 (1994)]; California Law Review, Stereotypes and Prejudice: Helping Legal Decisionmakers Break the Prejudice Habit [83 Cal. L. Rev. 733 (1995)].

# Negrophobia and Reasonable Racism

# "RATIONAL" DISCRIMINATION
# AND THE BLACK TAX

*It is a rainy night in a combined residential and commercial neighborhood in a predominantly White upper-middle-class section of a major U.S. city. It is 10:30 P.M. It is raining hard. Although most of the fashionable shops and boutiques in the neighborhood have closed, the neighborhood bank contains an automatic teller. The machine is located in a lobby between two sets of glass doors, the first of which opens directly into the bank and is locked at closing each day, while the second leads to the public sidewalk and remains open twenty-four hours.*

*A middle-aged resident of the neighborhood enters the bank's lobby, inserts her bank card into the machine, and requests two hundred dollars. As she waits for her transaction to be processed, the woman suddenly notices a figure moving directly toward the lobby from across the street. Focusing her full attention on the approaching figure, she notes that the per-son is a young man (at most twenty-something); that he is wearing a trench coat with an upturned collar and a tarpaulin hat pulled down even with his eyes (perhaps in deference to the pouring rain); and that he is Black.*

*The trench-coat-clad young man glances down the deserted street as he reaches the lobby and then enters, pushing his right shoulder against one of the swinging glass doors. As he pushes the door open, he unbuttons the collar of his trench coat with his right hand and reaches into the coat in the direction of his left armpit. With his eyes focused on the space beneath his coat into which he is reaching, he takes hold of something and begins to withdraw it.*

*Panic-stricken and conscious of the rhythmic clicking of the automatic teller churning out ten fresh twenty-dollar bills, the woman pulls a small .22 calibre pistol from her purse and lev-els it at the entering figure. As the young man looks up from his coat, he sees the pistol trained on him and reflexively thrusts his right hand—which now contains a billfold retrieved from his inside breast pocket—out in front of him, shouting at the woman not to shoot. Perceiving a handgun thrust in her direc-tion and startled by the man's unintelligible shouts, the woman shoots the Black man, who dies clutching his bank card.*

This troubling tableau taps the most disturbing source of dread in modern America—Black violence. Polls and studies repeat-edly show that most Americans believe that Blacks are "prone to violence." Anecdotal evidence points to the same conclusion. Many a would-be fare who happened to be Black has developed tennis elbow trying to flag down a taxi, incredulously watching as fellow White hailers are immediately picked up and whisked away. Further, as talk-show diva and media magnate Oprah Winfrey discovered when she was denied admittance to a tony boutique in Chicago that used a buzzer system to screen out "suspicious persons," even great fame and fantastic wealth do not guarantee immunity against Black stereotypes. As Stevie Wonder observed in one of his most trenchant lyrics, "You might make big cash/but you cannot cash in your face." And the face of crime, for many Americans, is Black.

In claiming self-defense, the shooter may argue that the Black victim's race is relevant to the reasonableness of her belief that she was about to be attacked. Her claim might be based on any of three distinct arguments. First, she could insist that it was reasonable to consider the victim's race in assessing the danger he posed because most people would do so. She might introduce studies or anecdotes demonstrating the frequency with which Americans make assumptions about an individual's character on the basis of race, and argue that she should not be punished for basing her response on the widely held belief that Blacks are more prone to be criminals than Whites. Second, she could point out that, independent of typical American beliefs, her consideration of the victim's race was reasonable because Blacks commit a disproportionate number of violent crimes and therefore pose a greater statistical threat. "Rational discrimination" would be her watchword. In framing this argument, she would show that large statistical differences exist between the crime rates of Blacks and non-Blacks, and she would assert that she knew of, and reasonably relied on, these statistical probabilities when deciding to shoot.

Finally, if the woman had previously been violently assaulted by a Black individual, she might maintain that her overreaction to the victim's race was reasonable in light of her earlier traumatic experience. One recent case accorded legal weight to such "Negrophobia" by holding that an ordinary person assaulted by an anonymous Black individual might develop a pathological fear of *all* Blacks sufficient to justify an award of disability benefits.[1] Invoking the same psychological proposition, our defendant might contend that her Negrophobia is relevant to the reasonableness of her reactions to the supposed assailant.

Because the concept of reasonableness drives self-defense doctrine, each of these race-based arguments might result in a determination that the shooter should be excused for shooting the Black bank customer. Indeed, recent experience shows that defendants in self-defense cases often exploit the racial fears of jurors in asserting the reasonableness of their fear of supposed assailants who are Black.[2] The meaning of race does not necessarily "speak for itself" in these cases; defense attorneys construe race in subtle and not-so-subtle ways with the goal of exonerating their clients. Homicide (and wrongful death) trials that center around race-based defenses, therefore, are telling crucibles in which to test the fairness of acting on racial fears.

To appreciate the growing acceptance of racially charged arguments of reasonableness in self-defense cases, one need go no further than the notorious New York subway vigilante case of *People v. Goetz*.[3] The defendant, Bernhard Goetz, successfully claimed that his shooting of four Black teenagers on a crowded subway after two of them smiled at him and "asked" for five dollars was justified as an act of self-defense. Goetz opened fire on the youths as soon as they "asked" for money, shooting some while they were retreating from the scene. He later confessed that he knew none of the youths had a gun. Goetz's defense attorney, Barry Slotnick, played on the racial factor throughout the trial, relentlessly characterizing the victims in subhuman, stereotype-laden terms such as "savages," "vultures," "predators on society."[4] The tactic worked. Goetz was acquitted by a predominantly White jury.

Exploitation of racial fears is also evident in the trial of the four White Los Angeles police officers who beat Rodney King. Although this was not strictly a self-defense case, public attention riveted on the White policemen's perception of the threat posed by an unarmed Black man. Throughout the trial, the defense teams made concerted efforts to portray King as an animal or monster. Indeed, one of the defendants, Stacey C. Koon, testified that King was "a monster-like figure akin to a Tasmanian devil."[5] In his closing argument, the attorney for defendant Laurence M. Powell stressed that the officers' blows were controlled efforts to subdue King, "a *Black* man" who was stopped for speeding, who tried to evade the police, and who only reluctantly complied with their commands.[6] How legitimate are such strategies? Consider first my bank ATM example.

Racial fears *are* legally relevant to the reasonableness of the shooter's reaction to the young Black man under self-defense doctrine, *technically*. Nevertheless, we must reject all her race-based claims of reasonableness. My concession that racial fears are "technically" relevant in self-defense doubtless will raise some eyebrows. "If he admits that on a formal level racial fears are legally relevant, but still rejects their acceptability," some will say, "then he must be willing to sacrifice logical consistency on the altar of political correctness." This objection reflects a specious but increasingly popular attack on antidiscrimination programs—formalism. A variety of pinched literalism that exalts form over substance, formalism holds that we look only at the letter of the law, disregarding its animating spirit, and that we equate people and situations that are superficially similar, ignoring deeper differences.

Many cries of "reverse discrimination" grow out of this fallacy: "If historically it was wrong for institutions to consider characteristics such as race and gender to *exclude* marginalized groups from core community activities, it is just as wrong for these institutions to consider such characteristics in affirmative efforts to *include* these same marginalized groups in these activities." Another aspect of the fallacy is the seemingly progressive "color-blind perspective" (or "color-blind formalism"). Under this perspective, decision makers—jurors, judges, employers, teachers, and so forth—must completely ignore race (as well as gender, sexual orientation, and any other markers of social marginality) when making social judgments of others. "Because historically race-consciousness has been used by bigots to oppress minorities," say advocates of the color-blind perspective, "it is racist and unjust for current-day decision makers to be race-conscious when making social judgments about Blacks (or women or gays and lesbians). Consciously thinking about race will lead either to discrimination against Blacks or to reverse discrimination in their favor." Formalism thus lumps situations together on the basis of some limited set of similarities and willfully ignores the very different interests, values, and social policies that distinguish them on a deeper level.

This book seeks to debunk such facile formalism. One vehicle for this debunking will be a comparison of the arguments made in defense of battered women who kill and those made in defense of minorities from "rotten social backgrounds" who kill. This comparison is especially needed in view of the O. J. Simpson trial and its rancorous aftermath. For, from the standpoint of popular reactions to the case, the trial seemed to pit the interests of one socially marginalized group, abused women, against those of another, Blacks. Trial watchers especially sensitive to injustices suffered by Blacks in the American justice system seemed more likely to endorse the acquittal, while those especially attuned to the plight of battered women seemed more likely to decry it.

Far from being antithetical, the interests of battered women and disadvantaged Blacks (and other minorities) coincide. At bottom, advocates for battered women and advocates for disadvantaged minorities must overcome the same entrenched conservative assumptions to successfully defend their respective clients. These assumptions bolster the subordination of women and impoverished Blacks by making their plight seem natural and just. We will trace the connections between their shared struggle against domination.

We will also examine recent research in human psychology that demonstrates that color-blind formalism—the effort to ignore a person's racial identity in making social judgments of her  promotes the very discrimination it professes to prevent. Decision makers who seek to reduce their biased judgments of stereotyped groups must practice color-consciousness, not color-blindness. Inculcation in color-blind orthodoxy is so firm and pervasive in this country, however, that many readers initially may need consciously to suspend disbelief in approaching this thesis. But I will build my argument for race-consciousness in social decision making on hard empirical proof, not faith.

A new numbers racket—discrimination by mathematics—

will be investigated as well. Defenders of "rational discrimination" (economist Walter Williams, columnist Richard Cohen,
pundit Dinesh D'Souza, and others) charge into discussions of
racial justice brandishing the sword of statistics about Black
crime rates, a weapon that upon closer inspection turns out to be
a hollow stage prop, a nerfsword. Careful analysis will reveal
not only that "rational discrimination" is not reasonable, it is
racist.

In exposing the "rational discrimination" canard, I will track
the formalistic impulse to what may be its most staunchly
defended bastion; namely, "high objectivity"—the assumption
that factual determinations and value judgments, like two separate tubs, sit on mutually independent bottoms. We will see
that, contrary to this assumption, formally identical factual
statements about the world, such as "I know my dog is leashed,"
cannot be treated the same when uttered in different situations.
Put differently, even if I have exactly the same factual information about my dog in two different situations, it may be reasonable for me to say "I know my dog is leashed" in one situation,
but totally unreasonable—even criminal—for me to say it in
another. In the end, therefore, by plumbing many unexamined
assumptions about law, justice, moral reasoning, human psychology, and "high objectivity," I hope to ferret out the injustices of formalism.

### Stubborn Optimism

My impetus for approaching the problem of racial discrimination from the standpoint of the American justice system comes
from experience. I first experienced the majesty of the law at age
eight when I was propelled from my sleep by a rude thunder-

clap. Still drowsy, I could feel the reverberations rumbling through our floorboards, swelling in intensity until they reached my bedroom door, which swung open on a man brandishing a shotgun and shouting, "Freeze—police!" What I mistook for a thunderclap turned out to be the sound of our front door unceremoniously parting company with its hinges and striking our living room floor. I first saw the door as my seven siblings and I were ushered into our family room to make room for the cops combing our apartment for contraband. As our gun-wielding escorts queued us up for a round of frisks, my eyes fastened on the blue serge suits hulking over my handcuffed and prostrate dad. I couldn't wait to see the looks on their mocking faces when my indomitable dad would snap off the handcuffs and send the cops scurrying for cover. But the next time I saw my dad upright and unshackled was on a Sunday, Family Day, in the Ohio State Penitentiary.

The five years of Family Days that followed gave me plenty of time to ponder the wonders of the law. What struck me as most wondrous about the law was how readily it could be manipulated by spiteful state officials against an innocent but "uppity" Black man. For innocent my dad most certainly was. Even as an eight-year-old I knew that a five-pound bag of marijuana could not spontaneously materialize from thin air in the kitchen cupboard where it was allegedly discovered. And even as an eight-year-old I knew my dad wasn't stupid or masochistic enough to stash it in the cupboard himself after a close friend in law enforcement had warned him a week earlier that we would be visited by Akron's finest that very night. So, ruling out spontaneous generation on the one hand and some kind of preposterous paternal "arrest wish" on the other, even to an eight-year-old the explanation was obvious: The grass was planted. (Scandals about persistent police frame-ups in Philadelphia, Los Angeles, and elsewhere, shocking to many, are old news to others.)[7]

Immersing himself in criminal procedure and constitutional law, drafting and filing his own writs and other legal memoranda, delivering his own oral arguments before appellate tribunals, my dad ultimately vindicated himself through federal habeas corpus, the legal procedure by which state prisoners can go to federal courts to argue that they were unconstitutionally convicted or sentenced (see *Armour v. Salisbury*, 492 F.2d 1032, 6th Cir. 1974). Sentenced as a *first*-time offender to twenty-two to fifty-five years for possession and sale of marijuana, he could still be wrongfully rotting in a jail cell if the current hostility to habeas had been in effect. The five years it took the slow wheels of justice to grind out his vindication, however, took a great toll, putting my mother on the public dole and resulting in the replacement of my dad's red brick high-rise apartment building—what he liked to call his "forty acres and a mule"—by a parking lot for *police* vehicles. Made the devil wanna holler!

The secret of my dad's popularity with the city fathers and guardians? As hinted earlier, for one thing he was an "uppity nigger." As history shows, "uppity nigger" is an appellation applied to Blacks who do not shuck and grin and walk on tippy-toes around certain Whites, literally or figuratively. Standing 6 feet 8 inches tall, weighing 260 pounds, possessing a better command of the Queen's English than most, blessed with keen business acumen, and flouting all the racial conventions of his day, my dad stood out as a Black Gulliver among the lily-White Lilliputians who controlled Akron's essentially segregated social, economic, and political institutions in the 1950s and 1960s.

But Dad was guilty of one affront even worse than uppity-ness, one many orders of magnitude more subversive of the racial caste system: miscegenation—the dread commingling of gene pools. Of course, the commingling of Black and White gene pools has a long history in the American experience. White male slave owners forcibly injected their genes into the Black population through the owners' rape of their Black female chattel for hundreds of years under slavery. But the thought of a 6 foot 8 inch barrel-chested Black man skinny-dipping in their European gene pool unhinged the "Lily-putians." (Recall, incredulous reader, that until the Supreme Court decision in *Loving v. Virginia* in 1967, in numerous Southern states interracial marriage was a crime. And certainly the racial attitudes that gave rise to the antimiscegenation laws in the South were not confined to Dixie; as Malcolm X put it: "Anything south of the Canadian border is 'The South.'") The rankling sight in the late 1950s and early 1960s of my Irish-American mom, with her head full of flaming red hair, and my strapping Black dad, kicking along main street in stride—one, two, arms locked, indubitably matched—undoubtedly contributed to his false imprisonment.

In college, I scoffed at the naiveté of my classmates who were applying to law schools with the stated objective of serving justice. In my view, entering a courtroom was like entering a crooked casino in which the decks are stacked, dice loaded, roulette wheels fiendishly rigged. It took my dad—who more than anyone had reason for cynicism—to disabuse me of my own. He hammered home that even though the Lily-putians had twisted the law to vent their own venomous prejudices, he himself had found redemption in the law, for he had found the key to his own jailhouse door in a lawbook of the prison library.

The law is not inherently racist or oppressive; it is merely a tool. It can serve as well as subvert justice. In the pages that follow I hope to draw on my dad's stubborn optimism to develop a more hopeful picture of the legal process than that drawn by some of its critics.

The primary reason for my cautious optimism about the future of the American justice system—despite its tragic history of racial injustice—is that I do not believe that most White people today are Lily-putians. Most White people today truly desire to be above racism. In this, I differ from some of my friends who hold that most Whites are incorrigibly prejudiced. Our hope for progress toward racial fairness in the courts and society, however, lies precisely in the empirically demonstrable desire of most Whites to promote egalitarian ideals and avoid invidious racial discrimination. The main challenge today is to forge a consensus about what constitutes racism and what to do about it.

### Racism on Stilts

Perhaps the gravest threat today to progress toward racial justice comes from the right-wing ideologues bent on convincing White people of good faith that negative stereotypes about Blacks are justified. Trotting out discredited studies, unscientific experiments, and cooked statistics, these pundits try to prove that Blacks are inherently less intelligent and more violent than Whites. The unmistakable implication of these "proofs" of Black inferiority is that disparities between Blacks and Whites in education and employment must be blamed on Blacks' own inferior genes, not on past and present discrimination. A further implication is that Whites need not resist the influence of some profoundly derogatory stereotypes on their thinking about Blacks. After all, according to these learned men, many of these ugly stereotypes are true!

Old-fashioned racism of the Ku Klux Klan variety is still out of fashion. Growing in its place, however, is the highbrow, pseudoscientific variety—racism on stilts, if you will—one that hides its fascist boots beneath a laboratory coat. Pseudoscientific apologies for racial subordination are nothing new in the American experience. One aim of this book is to add a nail to the coffin of this most recent embodiment of highbrow racism, though I am ever mindful that no quantity of nails will lay it to rest for good. For, like eighteenth-century body snatchers who made handsome profits stealing corpses from graves, opportunistic ideologues like Charles Murray and Richard Hernstein will always be prowling the cemeteries of science for the noisome remains of discredited scientific theories with which to foul the marketplace of ideas.

### The Black Tax

Consider what I will call the Black Tax. The Black Tax is the price Black people pay in their encounters with Whites (and some Blacks) because of Black stereotypes. The concept of a "tax" captures several key characteristics of these stereotype-laden encounters: like a tax, racial discrimination is persistent, pervasive, must be dealt with, cannot be avoided, and is not generally resisted. Taxes are commonly regarded as ineluctable facts of human existence, as in the old saw, "Nothing in life is certain save death and taxes." Racism, too, is regarded by many Black observers as inexorable, as reflected in Derrick Bell's "permanence of racism" thesis. And just as the state stands behind the collection of the general taxes, Blacks often have good cause to view state representatives such as police and judicial officers as IRS agents for the Black Tax.

The Black Tax has little to do with the Mark Fuhrman-style racism that led to the false imprisonment of my dad, however. The injuries inflicted on Blacks by avowedly virulent racists are grievous and still widespread, but as I suggested earlier, most Americans today are not Mark Fuhrmans, and thus most racial discrimination today is not rooted in conscious animus. Instead, most of it stems either from unconscious mental reflexes or from a belief that Blacks commit a disproportionate number of crimes and therefore statistically pose a greater threat than non-Blacks. It is unconscious discrimination on the one hand and ostensibly rational discrimination on the other that impose the lion's share of the Black Tax today.

The Black Tax comes in many varieties. Reports abound of Blacks being stopped and interrogated by police for walking or jogging through "White" neighborhoods. Police are often responding to calls from concerned neighbors. Although Fuhrman-style racism may lie behind such calls and stops, it is quite possible that these watchful callers and dutiful officers see themselves as responding reasonably to a person who seems to be "out of place"—nothing personal.

Likewise, it's "nothing personal" when store security personnel shadow Blacks in department stores, "nothing personal" when clerks refuse to buzz Blacks into jewelry stores and glitzy Manhattan boutiques, and when White women balk at getting on empty elevators with Black (but not White) men. Nothing personal, moreover, in profile stops of Blacks by drug enforcement officers, nothing personal in the redlining of Black neighborhoods by everything from banks to pizza delivery services, and positively nothing personal in the mountain of empirical evidence of racial discrimination in the administration of justice. Without a doubt, the shibboleth of today's apologists for the Black Tax is "nothing personal."

A serendipitous illustration of the attitude of many Whites toward the Black Tax emerged from my mailbox just as I was writing this Introduction. I opened the mail to find the following letter responding to remarks I made in a local newspaper, *The Pittsburgh Gazette,* in which I described the third degree of Blacks by suburban cops and the special attention I receive from store security personnel when I doff my business suit and don some sweats and sneakers.

Dear Mr. Armour:

Re your ramblings in yesterday's *Post-Gazette,* let me help you to understand.

If I saw blacks in my neighborhood I would be on the lookout, and for a good reason. In case your t.v. is broken, let me tell you what has been happening in western Pa., as well as the rest of the nation. Blacks, who represent about ten or eleven percent of the population are committing about seventy five percent of the crime. And, they are committing about ninety five percent of the street crimes. Just turn on the tube at night and see where the crimes are being carried out and by who.

When was the last time you heard about a drive-by shooting in Upper St. Clair [a predominantly White Pittsburgh suburb]? When is the last time you heard of a gang related killing in Fox Chapel [a predominantly White Pittsburgh suburb]? I think you got my point.

Of course sales people are going to watch blacks in a store more closely than whites. . . . Blacks commit a disproportionate amount of shop lifting. Hell, why do you think the large grocery stores have all but abandoned the inner cities where the population is mostly black?

I heard Jesse Jackson say that if he hears foot steps behind him and turns around to see a white face instead of a black one, he is relieved. Does that make him a racist? Does that make me a racist if I say the same thing? No, what it does is make a statement of fact.

Once, I would like to hear a black say he understands why whites feel the way we do. Please clean up your own home before you try to tell us how to think.

Without mincing words, the author of this letter bluntly states the case for the Black Tax from the standpoint of many White tax collectors. Especially telling is the authority the author cites for his statistics on Black criminality—television. Were television my sole source of information on violent crime, I might share the author's grim reckoning of relative racial crime rates. Thus I will investigate the role of the mass media in the perpetuation of the Black Tax. Sticking my head directly into the lion's mouth, I will also assume that—despite demonstrable biases in police enforcement—Blacks *do* commit a disproportionate number of street crimes and ask whether such a statistic justifies acceptance of the Black Tax either in the administration of justice or in the everyday interactions of ordinary citizens.

Further, I will focus on the most insidious and seemingly intractable source of the Black Tax: unconscious discrimination. Unlike the purportedly rational discrimination rooted in statistics, this variant resides in the inner recesses of the human psyche. Drawing on empirical studies, we will see that unconscious racial discrimination influences the social judgments of all Americans and lies at the heart of "Negrophobia," a posttraumatic stress disorder about Blacks that courts have actually permitted to play a role in formal legal proceedings.

Finally, not content to curse the gloom, I hope to light a candle. Specifically, I will frame a *proactive* strategy for helping individuals avoid imposing the Black Tax on African Americans. Using recent research in social and cognitive psychology, we will see how racially liberal people can combat unconscious discrimination by inhibiting their automatic negative responses to Blacks and replacing them with controlled, nonprejudiced ones. For this prejudice reduction strategy to work, individuals must consciously confront their own racial stereotypes. This is not easy. Courts, for example, are reluctant to allow attorneys to bring the issue of prejudice into the open at trial. Judges have barred attorneys who represent Blacks, gays, and other socially marginalized clients from encouraging jurors to confront their unconscious biases on the ground that such confrontations "play to the prejudices of the jury." Without proactive efforts, however, this most cruelly regressive of America's taxes will continue deepening this nation's racial rift; with such efforts, there is hope of healing.

I must add one caveat. I am no Pollyanna about the prospects for promoting social justice through the courts and other state institutions; the predations of the Leviathan state are too well known for such unqualified optimism. Unless one is possessed by an irresistible urge to assume the shape of a pancake, only a quixotic fool would charge head-on into an oncoming juggernaut—take it from a reformed flapjack. Yet I maintain that this juridic juggernaut called the American justice system can be gainfully wielded in the service of justice—but only by grasping its inner logic and, as in judo, using its own momentum against it. On this point, I share the sentiments of the influential nineteenth-century activist who exhorted, "We must force the frozen circumstances to dance by playing to them their own melody."

# Chapter One

# THE "REASONABLE RACIST": A SLIPPERY OXYMORON

The "Reasonable Racist" asserts that, even if his belief that Blacks are "prone to violence" stems primarily from racism—that is, from a belief in the genetic predisposition of Blacks toward greater violence, from uncritical acceptance of the Black cultural stereotype, or from personal racial animus—he should be excused for considering the victim's race before using force because most similarly situated Americans would have done so as well. In our criminal justice system, "blame is reserved for the (statistically) deviant,"[1] asserts the Reasonable Racist. "Therefore," he concludes, "an individual racist in a racist society cannot be condemned for an expression of human frailty as ubiquitous as racism."

The Reasonable Racist's position, though ultimately specious, can muster more factual and legal support than one might think.

With regard to his claim that average Americans share his fear of Black violence, the Reasonable Racist can point to evidence such as a 1990 University of Chicago study which found that more than one out of two Americans endorses the proposition that Blacks tend to be "violence prone."[2] Moreover, numerous recent news stories chronicle the widespread exclusion of Blacks from shops and taxicabs by anxious storekeepers and cabdrivers, many of whom openly admit to making race-based assessments of the danger posed by prospective patrons.[3] Thus, it is unrealistic to dispute the Reasonable Racist's depressing contention that Americans tend to associate violence with Black people.

That most Americans share the Reasonable Racist's discriminatory reactions to Blacks does not necessarily mean that they also share his racial prejudice. Many may claim to have completely nonracist grounds for their fear of Blacks. Specifically, many may insist that their racial fears are born of a sober analysis, or at least of rough intuition, of crime statistics that suggest Blacks commit a disproportionate number of violent street crimes. We shall consider such "rational racial fears" in the next chapter. Here we focus on irrational racial fears for two reasons. First, as we shall see in the discussion of unconscious mental reflexes in chapter 6, irrational factors figure to some extent in the racial fears of *all* Americans. Thus, just as he can prove that most Americans share his belief that Blacks are "prone to violence," the Reasonable Racist can also prove that, like him, most Americans harbor irrational responses to Blacks. Thus, his most controversial contention is that most Americans' heightened fear of Blacks is based *primarily* on conscious racial animus. This is equivalent to saying that most Americans are racist. I vigorously dispute this contention throughout this book.

The most apt description of the motivations that drive racial fears is "scrambled eggs." That is, racial fears rest on mixed motives, with the yolks of the rational impulses completely and seemingly inextricably commingled with the irrational whites. To probe the legal relevance of racial fears, these motives must be temporarily unscrambled and separately evaluated. If neither the irrational nor the rational motives can justify racial discrimination standing alone, there is no reason to recognize such discrimination when its underlying motives revert to their naturally scrambled state. Therefore, let us provisionally accept the Reasonable Racist's disquieting assumption that, like him, most Americans base their heightened fear of Black violence primarily on racism.

From the standpoint of legal doctrine, the Reasonable Racist also seems to have a case. Self-defense is generally defined as the use of a reasonable amount of force against another when the defender honestly and *reasonably* believes that she is about to be attacked, and that she must use such force to repel the attack.[4] To be excused, then, the shooter in our tableau must convince the jury that she honestly and reasonably believed that she had to shoot just when she did to avoid being killed or seriously injured, and that nothing less drastic than deadly force would have saved her.[5]

Reasonableness is the linchpin of legal self-defense in two respects. First, even if the defender is mistaken in her belief that she is under attack (as was the shooter in the tableau), she has a valid defense as long as her mistaken belief was reasonable.[6] Second, from a juror's perspective, the reasonableness of a belief is a window on its honesty; that is, the more reasonable the belief seems to a jury, the more likely a jury is to be convinced that the defendant honestly held the belief herself. In the law of self-defense, therefore, "reasonableness" is the pivotal standard to which all other legal requirements are related and by which all others are measured.

The Reasonable Racist's case hinges, therefore, on whether he can establish that typical beliefs are reasonable beliefs. The notion that typical beliefs are reasonable finds legal expression in certain familiar personifications of the reasonableness requirement, such as "the ordinary prudent man," "the average man," "the man in the street,"[7] and "the man who takes the magazines at home, and in the evening pushes the lawn mower in his shirt sleeves."[8] The layreader must understand that "reasonableness" in legal discourse is a term of art, that is, a word whose legal usage differs markedly from that of ordinary language. A "reasonable" attitude or belief in legal discourse is not necessarily rational or right from some objective, eye-in-the-sky point of view. Instead, as the "average man" formulation of the reasonableness standard suggests, courts tend to equate reasonable beliefs and attitudes with *typical* beliefs and attitudes. In the words of one criminal law expert, the Reasonable Man "is more appropriately described as the Ordinary Man (i.e., a person who possesses ordinary human weaknesses)."[9] Moreover, in practically applying the reasonable person standard, the jurors—themselves typical people holding typical beliefs—ordinarily judge the reasonableness of the defendant's beliefs by projecting themselves into the defendant's situation and asking whether they would have shared his beliefs under similar circumstances. If the answer is yes, the Reasonable Racist maintains, the defendant should prevail.

### How We Know What We Know: The Typical, the Reasonable, and the Accurate

Typical beliefs may be considered reasonable for two very different reasons. First, they are presumed to be accurate.[10] Most of our claims to knowledge about the world rest on typical beliefs; we assume that the propositions about the world that "everyone knows" (propositions often equated with "common sense") are true unless we have reason to doubt them. Of course, common sense may reflect and perpetuate oppressive myths and expedient misconceptions. Many women died excruciating deaths several hundred years ago because of the typical belief that witches cast spells that poisoned well water and caused crop failures. To see the disturbing implications for self-defense doctrine of the deep-seated assumption that typical beliefs are accurate, we need only make a few modifications in our earlier hypothetical situation and place it in the first half of the seventeenth century, the height of witch burnings in Europe:

*The owner of a general store is counting his lucre at day's end when out of the corner of his eye he suddenly notices a figure approaching his store. Focusing his full attention on the approaching figure, he notes that the person is an old woman (at least 65); that she is wearing a black dress and a cone-shaped black hat; and that she has a wart on her nose. As the old woman crosses the threshold, she reaches toward a pouch on a string around her neck (where she keeps her money, to buy something from the storekeeper) but which the storekeeper thinks is a pouch for potions. Panic-stricken and conscious of the bad graces he is in with the old women of the town (he has never passed up an opportunity to bilk or insult one he came across), he pulls a crossbow from under his counter and levels it at the entering figure. Seeing the crossbow trained on her, the woman thrusts her right hand in front of her while shouting at the man not to release the arrow. Perceiving spell-inducing gesticulations and unintelligible incantations, the storekeeper shoots and kills the old woman, who dies clutching a gold ducat.*

However disturbing it may seem, in a seventeenth-century court that indulged the still prevalent presumption of accuracy for typical beliefs, there is no reason to think the storekeeper's self-defense claim would not pass muster. Yet, despite the long and deplorable litany of injustices that historically have sprung from blind faith in conventional wisdom, conservatives continue to tout the sovereignty of "common sense" (Oliver North calls his syndicated talk show "common sense radio—for all America," and Philip Howard's book, *Death of Common Sense*, has been celebrated by conservatives for its catchy title, even though its substance does not necessarily bolster the conservative agenda).

American courts have shown undue deference to typical beliefs even in the case of scientific knowledge, an area where one would hope for a more searching truth-seeking methodology than mere nose counting. Until very recently, the test courts adopted for determining whether an expert could give an opinion on a scientific matter was whether the expert's methodology and conclusions were consistent with the consensus of the scientific community. In other words, courts would not permit experts to talk about theories and findings that were not *typical* for the scientific community. The courtroom doors were closed to cutting-edge iconoclasts—contemporary counterparts of Copernicus and Galileo were denied a voice in the high halls of justice. Opinions that did not conform to prevailing scientific paradigms and practices were essentially treated as "junk science." Such judicial genuflection to scientific orthodoxy has abated somewhat following the Supreme Court's 1993 *Daubert* decision, in which the Court rejected the "general acceptance" test for scientific evidence in federal courts.[11] Nevertheless, the pitfalls of relying too heavily on conventional wisdom, "common sense," and hoary tradition in the search for truth can hardly be overstated.

Whether the reference group for determining what is typical is society at large (as in the case of the witch burnings) or some privileged subgroup within society (as in the case of the scientific community for purposes of expert testimony), our legal system tends to reward conformity and penalize nonconformity with the majority. Certainly the reasonableness standard, in its classic legal formulations (e.g., the "average man"), privileges the perspective of the majority. This approach to reasonableness might be equated to the problem of the Procrustean bed. In Greek mythology, Procrustes was a highwayman who waylaid unsuspecting travelers and dragged them to his lair, where he bound them to his bed. Although the abducted travelers came in many different sizes, Procrustes' bed came in only one. If a hapless traveler proved too short for his host's bed, Procrustes racked and stretched him into conformity; too long, Procrustes lopped of the offending extremities. In the end, the diversity of dimensions that the different travelers embodied was reduced to bland uniformity—a consummation devoutly sought by current proponents of Procrustean legislation that is fashioned to force the body politic to speak only one language, form only one kind of sexual union, worship only one god, and embrace only one worldview.

Procrustean beds abound in the law, but perhaps nowhere more than in the legal definition of reasonableness, which figures centrally in such areas as torts, contracts, criminal law, and criminal procedure. The legal definition of reasonableness is uniquely insidious in that it takes the merely typical and contingent and presents it as truth and morality, objectively construed. For example, according to legal usage, the "objective" standard of reasonableness encompasses those beliefs and attitudes that are shared by most people. In those limited instances in which a court instructs a jury to look at a situation from the standpoint of an actor's atypical beliefs and attitudes, it is said to apply a "subjective" standard of reasonableness. Thus, a battered woman may believe that calling the police or attempting to separate from her batterer will only put her in greater danger. Accordingly, she may shoot him in his sleep. In judging the reasonableness of her belief, typical jurors may believe that calling the police or walking out would have prevented further harm. Some courts would characterize the jurors' beliefs in this case as the "objectively" reasonable ones, while they would admit evidence of the battered woman's atypical beliefs (especially expert testimony about those beliefs) only under the "subjective" test of reasonableness.

The problem with this approach is that the battered woman's beliefs may be decidedly more rational and accurate than the jurors'. The beliefs of ordinary jurors about battering relationships are often based on inexperience and naiveté, or on ideological suppositions that women who remain in battering relationships masochistically enjoy being beaten, deserve to be beaten, or at least assume the risk of beatings. Saying that the wrongheaded beliefs of typical jurors meet the "objective" standard of reasonableness, while the atypical but accurate and rational beliefs of the battered woman are only relevant under a "subjective" standard of reasonableness, disparages the woman's beliefs and wrenches all recognizable meaning from the term "objective."

In the end, typical beliefs—in courts and in everyday life—still carry with them a presumption of accuracy. Accordingly, typical beliefs about the propensity of Blacks toward violence are deemed reasonable (i.e., accurate) insofar as we have no reason to doubt them. Often, however, a racially sensitive defender will not be claiming that his fearful reaction to Blacks is rational, but merely excusable. I therefore turn to the legal relation between the typical and the excusable.

### Why We Blame Whom We Blame: The Typical, the Reasonable, and the Damnable

Alternatively, typical beliefs may be considered reasonable on the supposition that they are not blameworthy, however inaccurate or even irrational they may be.[12] This is the claim of reasonableness invoked by both the Reasonable Racist and, as we will discuss later, the Involuntary Negrophobe. According to this position, even admittedly wrong judgments about a fact or situation should be excused so long as most people would have reached the same wrong conclusions under similar circumstances. A roll of keys that looks just like a gun in the eerily flickering lights of a bank lobby provides a simple illustration of this excuse. The argument rests on the premise that "blame is reserved for the (statistically deviant); we are blamed only for those actions and errors in judgment that others would have avoided."[13] Under a noninstrumental theory of criminal liability (that is, a theory that determines legal liability solely on the basis of an actor's just deserts, and that gives no weight to social policy in fixing liability), it is unjust to punish someone like the Reasonable Racist since his typical beliefs are by definition not morally blameworthy.[14]

Speaking to a jury of other seventeenth-century men, the storekeeper who shot the supposed witch would argue that his belief was typical and accurate; speaking to a modern jury, however, he might concede that his beliefs were inaccurate, but still argue that they were typical for someone from his cultural background, and that therefore he was not blameworthy for holding such admittedly inaccurate beliefs. When the reference group for determining whether an attitude or belief is typical is not the majority, this kind of claim is referred to as the "cultural defense." Thus, a Hmong tribesman from Laos kidnapped his intended bride in California and raped her in order to officiate their marriage, as is the tradition in his native country.[15] Also in California, a Chinese mother killed her son in an attempt to commit parent-child suicide after discovering her husband's adultery.[16] Through a "cultural defense," these defendants could attempt to negate or mitigate their criminal liability by arguing that they believed they were reasonably committing such acts because their cultural background and beliefs permit, and even encourage, such behavior.

Of course, insofar as our courts reject the claims of these cultural minorities, they raise Procrustean bed concerns. But insofar as they recognize such claims, they raise the problems on which the discussion now centers, namely, the problem of showing undue deference—and giving undue normative legitimacy—to the merely typical. Our investigations will uncover more such conundrums as we proceed.

A variant of the cultural defense is often asserted in defense of some of this country's revered "forefathers." For example, not long ago I heard a Black alumnus of the University of Virginia singing the illimitable praises of his alma mater's founder and benefactor, Thomas Jefferson. "You know, Jefferson maintained that Blacks were a naturally inferior race and remained a slave owner until the day he died," I observed.[17] "Oh, but it is unfair to judge him by today's standards," my interlocutor shot back. "Lots of people owned slaves back then, and most Americans of that era thought it was all right. Besides, Jefferson was a gentleman slaver." I was about to respond that a "gentleman slaver" is like a "nice Nazi," but it occurred to me that such a point would not assail the logic of his position—if anti-Semitism was a typical attitude among Germans in the 1930s and 1940s, how could we by his logic blame individual Germans of that era for holding such typical attitudes?

The problem with the claim that typical attitudes are not blameworthy is easier to recognize in cultural-defense cases, where what is typical for the cultural minority is not typical for the majority, than in cases where what we mean by typical beliefs and values are our very own cherished majoritarian beliefs and values. Acknowledging that our own typical values and beliefs may not reflect absolute truth and justice raises problems of moral and epistemological relativity that many of us would rather avoid honestly confronting. This is why the popular movie *Pulp Fiction*, though widely touted as iconoclastic, is at its core highly conservative. Early in the movie, the John Travolta character revels in cultural relativity by regaling his cohort in crime, played by Samuel L. Jackson, with stories of the different standards employed in different countries: a different system of weights and measures in France, and different, more permissive drug laws in Amsterdam. Jackson's character revels in the relativity as well, until he partakes of a burger called The Big Kahuna (Big Kahuna is the Hawaiian phrase for high priest), after which he "gets religion." When Travolta is invited to partake of The Big Kahuna, however, he declines. Travolta's refusal to renounce relativism leads to his demise (the price of relativism is death). Jackson, thanks to his espousal of absolutism, dodges the bullet. In the end, *Pulp Fiction* offers moviegoers relief from the vertiginous relativity of post-modernism via conversion to Judeo-Christian dogma . . . follow you who can.

But America is a diverse nation, many of whose members do not subscribe to any monolithic code of moral absolutism and harbor healthy skepticism toward those who profess to have a privileged pipeline to some God's-eye view of truth and justice. Moreover, this country is officially irreligious by constitution. Consequently, are there any coherent grounds upon which to build a critique of the claims of the Reasonable Racist? Is it even possible, let alone just, to discipline a person for beliefs, attitudes, and reactions that they share with most of the people around them, without either appealing to moral absolutes or somehow bootstrapping oneself to a position outside the prevailing belief system and into a God's-eye perspective?

In contrast to an "externalist" critique, which seeks a God's-eye perspective on a set of beliefs and reactions, a more coherent critique draws from an "internalist" perspective by seeking leverage for its critical evaluations from within the belief system itself. An internalist approach criticizes a belief or practice by showing how it contradicts or undermines other important beliefs, practices, values, and convictions within the same belief system. The values of the belief system need not have been handed down from some divine oracle, but rather may evolve gradually from historical processes and political struggles. The high value American culture places on free speech, for example, cannot be deduced from the Ten Commandments, and it took a bloody civil war for antislavery values to take root fully in our cultural belief system.[18] Democratic struggle over moral and legal definitions, on the one hand, and exposure of contradiction and hypocrisy, on the other—these are the defining characteristics of the internalist approach.

Legal disputes in our justice system are argued and resolved within an internalist perspective. Parties to a legal dispute, whether over ownership of a parcel of land or school desegregation, couch their contentions in terms of moral norms and social policies for which there is significant support in society's moral and legal discourse. Thurgood Marshall did not argue *Brown v. Board of Education*, the landmark school desegregation case, by appealing to some critical morality that lacked roots in the social morality and legal discourse of his times. Instead, he relentlessly hammered home the contradiction between segregation and deep-seated American moral and legal convictions. Applying an internalist methodology, he—like my incarcerated father—found a way to "make the frozen circumstances dance by playing to them their own melody."

Social morality—as distinct from popular morality—provides a basis for critiquing even widely shared beliefs and attitudes. Social morality consists of moral standards rooted in aspirations for the community as a whole, and that can fairly be said to have substantial support in the community or can be derived from norms that have such support.[19] "Popular morality," on the other hand, consists of moral norms that reflect a majority of opinion about appropriate behavior at some particular point in time. Despite considerable overlap between social morality and the popular version, they are *not* coextensive. Popular opinions about morally acceptable behavior feed social morality, but social morality is a river fed by many streams. A nation's constitutional promises, for example, contribute to its social morality, even when that nation, seized by popular prejudices and opinions about morally acceptable behavior, breaks those promises for a period of time, as it did when the United States interned Japanese Americans in concentration camps during World War II. That the United States has officially repented of its wartime treatment of Japanese Americans and offered monetary restitution for its transgressions points to its own realization that popular judgments of appropriate behavior at a given time may contradict deeper norms and convictions that the formerly popular judgments dismissed too lightly.

Indeed, most constitutional provisions work this way—they are promises a body politic makes to itself, ideally at the behest of its nobler impulses and "higher angels," which it hopes will protect its better self from a later weaker or less just self; they are the ropes Ulysses uses to bind himself to the mast to help him resist the siren songs he knows await him. Sadly, however, given the Supreme Court's recent assault on the Bill of Rights, which has been significantly fueled by the very fear of Black crime that we are considering, it appears that some of Ulysses' robed shipmates are bent on hacking away at his self-imposed coils in the name of siren justice.

Once the relationship between social and popular morality is properly understood, it is easier to see the flaw in the claim of the Reasonable Racist. The Reasonable Racist assumes that the sole function of the reasonable-man test is to reflect popular morality and that the sole objective of the legal system is to punish those who deviate from popular attitudes and beliefs. The role of the courts, from this perspective, is to *observe* rather than *define* the attributes of the reasonable man.

Whether courts that apply the reasonable-man standard should merely accommodate prevailing attitudes and practices or instead actively channel them in directions that serve higher social interests is a long-standing legal debate. In the famous torts case of *T. J. Hooper*,[20] for example, a defendant tug owner argued that the reasonableness of his decision not to equip his tug with a safety device should be judged on the basis of the behavior of most other tug owners. Because most other tug owners also failed to install the safety devices, the defendant argued, his failure to install them should be deemed reasonable. Judge Learned Hand, writing for the court, refused to equate the reasonable with the typical, however. Making it clear that courts do not merely observe, but actively define standards of reasonable behavior, Hand held: "[I]n most cases reasonable prudence is in fact common prudence; but strictly is never its measure; a whole calling may have unduly lagged in the adoption of new and available devices. . . . Courts must in the end say what is required; *there are precautions so imperative that even their universal disregard will not excuse their omission.*" Hand's recognition that courts have a duty to actively define standards and thereby channel social behavior applies with equal force to both civil and criminal cases.[21]

This analysis exposes the fallacy of equating reasonableness with typicality. Even if the "typical" American believes that Blacks' "inherent propensity" toward violence justifies a quicker and more forceful response when a suspected assailant is Black, this fact is legally significant only if the law defines *reasonable* beliefs as *typical* beliefs. The reasonableness inquiry, however, extends beyond typicality to consider moral standards rooted in aspirations for the community as a whole. Even when such moral standards are ignored by most of a community, it is incumbent upon the courts, as trustees of these higher standards, to hold the community accountable to them.

Avoidance of invidious racial discrimination has achieved the hard-won status of a core value in this nation's social morality. Support for this value can be readily found in sources ranging from constitutional provisions and legislative decrees to newspaper editorials. Accordingly, courts must not allow an attribute like irrational racial bias to figure in the formulation and application of the reasonable-man standard, however widespread that attribute may be. Although in most cases the beliefs and reactions of typical people reflect what may fairly be expected of a particular actor, this is not always true. "Should" must never be confused with "is," no matter how widespread what "is" may be. "Nice Nazis," "gentlemen slavers," and Reasonable Racists—this troika of odious oxymorons—stand as cautionary reminders of the danger of smug complacency in the face of what "is."

# Chapter Two

# THE "INTELLIGENT BAYESIAN": RECKONING WITH RATIONAL DISCRIMINATION

There is nothing more painful to me at this stage in my life than to walk down the street and hear footsteps and start thinking about robbery—then look around and see somebody White and feel relieved.

—The Reverend Jesse Jackson, in a speech to a Black congregation in Chicago decrying Black-on-Black crime

White America craves absolution. At least according to *U.S. News & World Report* it does. By admitting he sometimes fears young Black men, the Reverend Jackson "seemed to be offering sympathetic Whites something for which they hungered: absolution," declared *U.S. News.*[1] For other journalists, Jackson's comments were as much about vindication as absolution—in their view, his comments put an acceptable face on their own discriminatory beliefs and practices. Richard Cohen of the *Washington Post*, for example, announced in his column that Jackson's remarks "pithily paraphrase what I wrote" in 1986.[2] He was referring to a 1986 column in which he asserted that if he were a shopkeeper, he would lock his doors "to keep young Black men out." For Cohen, Jackson's remarks proved that "it is not racism to recognize a potential threat posed by someone with certain characteristics."

Cohen's advocacy of discrimination against young Black men raises a second argument advanced to justify acting on race-based assumptions, namely, that, given statistics demonstrating Blacks' disproportionate engagement in crime, it is reasonable to perceive a greater threat from someone Black than someone White. Walter Williams, a conservative Black economist, refers to someone like Cohen as an "Intelligent Bayesian," named for Sir Thomas Bayes, the father of statistics.[3] For Williams, stereotypes are merely statistical generalizations, probabilistic rules of thumb that, when accurate, help people make speedy and often difficult decisions in a world of imperfect information. Whether "intelligent" is an apt adjective for a person who discriminates on the basis of stereotypes remains to be seen. For now we shall simply refer to such a person as a "Bayesian."

On its surface, the contention of the Bayesian appears relatively free of the troubling implications of the Reasonable Racist's defense. While the Reasonable Racist explicitly admits his prejudice and bases his claim for exoneration on the prevalence of irrational racial bias, the Bayesian invokes the "objectivity" of numbers. The Bayesian's argument is simple: "As much as I regret it, I must act differently toward Blacks because it is logical to do so." The Bayesian relies on numbers that reflect not the prevalence of racist attitudes among Whites, but the statistical disproportionality with which Blacks commit crimes.

As with any school of thought, Bayesians range from the vulgar to the more refined. An example of a vulgar Bayesian is Michael Levin, a social philosopher, who uses statistics to argue that a person jogging alone after dark is morally justified in fearing a young Black male ahead of him on a jogging track:

It is widely agreed that young Black males are significantly more likely to commit crimes against persons than are members of any other racially identifiable group. Approximately one Black male in four is incarcerated at some time for the commission of a felony, while the incarceration rate for White males is between 2 and 3.5%.

. . . Suppose, jogging alone after dark, you see a young Black male ahead of you on the running track, not attired in a jogging outfit and displaying no other information-bearing trait. Based on the statistics cited earlier, you must set the likelihood of his being a felon at 25. . . . On the other hand it would be rational to trust a White male under identical circumstances, since the probability of his being a felon is less than .05. Since whatever factors affect the probability of the Black attacking you—the isolation, your vulnerability—presumably affect the probability of a White attacking you as well, it remains more rational to be more fearful of the Black than of the White.[4]

Levin erroneously suggests that because one out of four Black men is incarcerated for commission of a felony, the statistical benchmark a person should use in judging the risk of violent assault posed by a randomly selected young Black man is 25 percent. Levin's statistics, however, say only that one in four Black males is incarcerated for *a* felony, not that one in four is incarcerated for a violent felony. Only the proportion of Blacks incarcerated for *violent* felonies can provide any kind of benchmark for judging relative risks of violent assault by race. But the typical African American male in the criminal justice system is *not a violent offender*.[5] Most of the increase in the number of Blacks in the criminal justice system is attributable to the "War on Drugs" and stepped-up crackdowns on drug crimes.[6] In fact, the majority of arrestees for violent offenses are White.[7]

Assuming the woman who shot the suspected robber is a more refined Bayesian, she might frame her argument as follows. Although Blacks only make up 12 percent of the population, they are arrested for 62 percent of armed robberies.[8] Therefore, the *rate* of robbery arrests among Blacks is approximately twelve times the rate among non-Blacks. In other words, if a defender had to make a purely race-based assessment of the risk of armed robbery, it would be approximately twelve times more probable that any given Black person is a robber than a non-Black.[9] Even assuming considerable bias in police arrests, the refined Bayesian might conclude, no one can honestly say that actual rates of robbery by race are even close.

One can concede the Bayesian's point that the rates of robbery by race are "not close" and still ask, "So what?" It is far from clear what sorts of group-based robbery rates would justify the judgment that any given member of the group presents a sufficiently high risk of robbery to be deemed "suspicious." To make the point a different way, imagine I have two drawers, one white and the other black. Into the white drawer I pour one thousand marbles, 999 of which are green and one of which is red. Into the black drawer I also pour one thousand marbles, but this time I included twelve times the number of red ones. Thus the black drawer contains twelve red and 988 green marbles, or slightly over 1 percent red marbles. Twelve times a very small fraction may still be a very small fraction.

Now, substitute the social groups "Whites" and "Blacks" for the white and black drawers respectively, make the red marbles the members of each group arrested for violent crimes, and the problem with reading too much into the relative rates of robbery by race becomes evident. Blacks arrested for violent crimes comprised less than 1 percent of the Black population in 1994, and only 1.86 percent of the Black male population.[10] Recall that even a vulgar Bayesian like Levin—who equates being incarcerated with being incarcerated for a violent crime—asserts that because the incarceration rate for White males is between 2 and 3.5 percent, "it would be rational to trust a White male" you see ahead of you while jogging alone after dark. By this Bayesian's own logic, therefore, since Blacks arrested for violent crimes make up less than 1.9 percent of the Black male population, "it would be rational to trust a [Black] male" you ran into in the dark.

Let's assume—perhaps erroneously—that the rates of robbery by race are in some marginal sense "statistically significant." Thus, the Bayesian asserts that he would never employ race as the sole or even dominant risk factor in assessing someone's dangerousness. "I merely seek to give race its correct incremental value in my calculations," he assures us with all the aplomb of Mr. Spock. Thus, in addition to race, he carefully weighs other personal characteristics—such as youth, gender, dress, posture, body movement, and apparent educational level—before deciding how to respond. Having tallied up these "objective" indices of criminality, the Intelligent Bayesian argues that his conduct was reasonable (and thus not morally blameworthy) because it was "rational."

A threshold problem with the Bayesian's profession of pristine rationality concerns the "scrambled eggs" problem described earlier—that is, the practical impossibility of unscrambling the rational and irrational sources of racial fears. For countless Americans, fears of Black violence stem from, among other things, the complex interaction of cultural stereotypes, racial antagonisms, and unremitting overrepresentations of Black violence in the mass media. As for the mass media, especially television news, recall the letter in the Introduction from the would-be Bayesian who remarked, "If I saw Blacks in my neighborhood I would be on the lookout, and for a good reason." The "good reason" he cites for his hypervigilance about Blacks is television. Few Americans keep copies of FBI Uniform Crime Reports by their bedsides: when asked in a *Los Angeles Times* survey (February 13, 1994) from where they got their information about crime, 65 percent of respondents said they learned about it from the mass media. But television journalism on crime and violence has been proven to reveal, and project, a consistent racial bias.[11]

Even if media reporting on crime and violence were not biased, our minds simply do not process information about Blacks and other stereotyped groups the way the Bayesian assumes. The Bayesian assumes that our minds can passively mirror the world around us, that they can operate like calculators, and that social stereotypes can be represented in our minds as mere bits of statistical information, as malleable and subject to ongoing revision as the batting averages of active major-league baseball players. Each of these assumptions flies in the face of what modern psychology reveals about the workings of the human mind.

As is described in detail in chapter 6, social stereotypes are not mere bits of statistical information but rather well-learned sets of associations among groups and traits established in children's memories before they reach the age of judgment. And once a stereotype becomes entrenched in our memory, it takes on a life of its own. Case studies have demonstrated that once an individual internalizes a cultural stereotype, she unconsciously interprets experiences to be consistent with the underlying stereotype, selectively assimilating facts that validate the stereotype while disregarding those that do not.[12] The tendency of individuals to reject or ignore evidence that conflicts with their cultural stereotypes expresses itself in many forms, perhaps none as perplexing as the backhanded "compliment" some White liberals think appropriate to bestow on "deserving" Blacks: "I don't think of you as Black." For Blacks who harbor the hope that their personal achievements can "uplift the race" by upending stereotypes, these clumsy bouquets are deeply disturbing. The more success you achieve, the *less* likely that your success will redound to the reputational benefit of your community. In the words of Evelyn Lewis, the first Black woman to make partner in a major San Francisco law firm, "[W]hat you do well will reflect well on you, but only as an individual. And what you do poorly—well, that's when what you do will be dumped on the whole race."[13] To the extent that the Bayesian aggressively assimilates negative statistical information about Blacks while remaining oblivious to contradictory or positive statistical information, she undermines her claim of objectivity.

Further, the Bayesian's contention that she can delicately balance the racial factor in her calculations is refuted by recent discoveries about the psychological impact of stereotypes. A stereotype, unlike ordinary statistical information, radically alters our mindset, unconsciously bringing about a sea change in our perceptual readiness. Under the influence of a stereotype, we tend to see *what the stereotype primes us to see*. If violence is part of the stereotype, we are primed to construe ambiguous behavior as evincing violence, not on a retail but on a wholesale level. Thus, even if race marginally increases the probability that an "ambiguous" person is an assailant, decision makers inevitably exaggerate the *weight* properly accorded to this fact. Whatever merit there is to the contention that it is appropriate to consider a person's race as one—just one—of the factors defining the "kind" of person who poses a danger, the racial factor assumes overriding psychological significance when the supposed assailant is Black.

For White Bayesians, cultural differences increase the danger of overestimating the threat posed by a supposed Black assailant. Nonverbal cues such as eye contact and body communication, for instance, vary significantly among subcultures, and thus may fail in intercultural situations.[14] If the female bank patron in our opening hypothetical scenario were White (her racial identity is intentionally undefined), her misinterpretation of the Black victim's eye and body movements as furtive and threatening may have resulted from cultural differences in nonverbal cues, illogically distorting her perception of danger.

Even if we accept the Bayesian's insistence that his greater fear of Blacks results wholly from unbiased analysis of crime statistics, biases in the criminal justice system undermine the reliability of the statistics themselves. Racial discrimination in sentencing, for example, causes arrest statistics to exaggerate what differences might exist in crime patterns between Blacks and Whites, thus undermining the reliability of such statistics.[15] A 1996 New York State study revealed that 30 percent of Blacks and Hispanics received harsher sentences than Whites in New York for comparable crimes, and that approximately four thousand Blacks and Hispanics are incarcerated each year for crimes under circumstances that do not lead to incarceration for Whites. Further exaggerating differences between Black and White crime rates is discrimination by police officers in choosing whom to arrest.[16] Thus, although the rate of robbery arrests among Blacks is approximately twelve times that of Whites, it does not necessarily follow that a particular Black person is twelve times more likely to be a robber than a White.

Although biases in the criminal justice system exaggerate the differences in rates of violent crime by race, it may, tragically, still be true that Blacks commit a disproportionate number of crimes. Given that the blight of institutional racism continues to disproportionately limit the life chances of African Americans, and that desperate circumstances increase the likelihood that individuals caught in this web may turn to desperate undertakings, such a disparity, if it exists, should sadden but not surprise us. As Guido Calabresi, former dean of the Yale Law School and current federal appeals court judge, points out: "[O]ne need not be a racist to admit the possibility that the stereotypes may have some truth to them. I don't believe in race, but if people are treated badly in a racist society on account of an irrelevant characteristic such as color or language, it should not be surprising if they react to that treatment in their everyday behavior."[17]

The media spin on the comments of the Reverend Jackson decrying Black-on-Black crime used Jackson's call for Blacks to take action on crime in their communities as an admission by the civil rights leader that racism and economic injustice have nothing to do with the crime problems of those communities. Columnist Mike Royko, for example, reported that Jackson believes it's "a waste of time to expect government to reduce . . . urban mayhem."[18] From this standpoint, self-help and government investment are mutually exclusive. Anyone advocating antibias programs or federal aid to cities is portrayed as "making excuses" for Black people's own self-destructiveness. Accordingly, when Jackson expressed fear that his ideas would be misconstrued by media and politicians looking for scapegoats, and further reiterated his long-standing insistence that *both* government help and self-help are needed for the African American community, he was widely derided. "[R]ather than grant [Whites the absolution for which they hungered]—and reap the enormous good will and political cooperation such a move might bring—Jackson has pulled back," declared *U.S. News*.[19]

To the extent that Blacks do commit disproportionate numbers of violent street crimes, socioeconomic status largely explains such overrepresentation. Crime rates are inextricably linked to poverty and unemployment. Genetic explanations of crime statistics founder on the fact that crime and delinquency rates of the African American middle class are virtually identical to those of Whites similarly situated.[20]

Recognizing the socioeconomic factors that drive violent street crime, the Bayesian may insist that he views race merely as a proxy for information with admittedly greater predictive value—such as income, education, and prospects for the future—but that costs more to obtain. "Thus," says the Bayesian, "I consider a wealthy Black graduate of the Harvard Law School who is making six figures at a major Wall Street law firm to pose a lower risk of armed robbery than a poor and illiterate White high school dropout with little hope of gainful employment."

"However," he continues, "ascertaining an individual's schooling and income may require a personal interview and reference checks. The costs of obtaining such particularized information may be prohibitive in many situations. Surely you can't expect shopkeepers, cabdrivers, or people in the position of our hypothetical bank patron to incur such costs, to get a person's life story before he fingers his buzzer, stops his taxi, or uses deadly defensive force against a 'suspicious' person. When obtaining such information is prohibitively costly, we must economize by using stereotypes and playing the odds."

Viewed in this light, the Bayesian's claim that race can serve merely as a proxy for socioeconomic status might seem persuasive. But if race is a proxy for socioeconomic factors, then race loses its predictive value when one controls for those factors. Thus, if an individual is walking through an impoverished, "crime-prone neighborhood," as the Reverend Jackson may have had in mind, and if he has already weighed the character of the neighborhood in judging the dangerousness of his situation, then it is illogical for him to consider the racial identity of the person whose suspicious footsteps he hears. For he has already taken into account the socioeconomic factors for which race is a proxy, and considering the racial identity of the ambiguous person under such circumstances constitutes "double counting."[21]

Since our hypothetical scenario takes place in a predominantly White upper-middle-class neighborhood, it does not seem to implicate the double-counting problem. Further, the discussion shall proceed on the basis of two assumptions: first, that the rate of robberies is "significantly" higher for Blacks than for non-Blacks; second, and most unrealistic, that the defendant's greater fear of Blacks results entirely from his analysis of crime statistics. Given these assumptions, what objections to the argument of the Bayesian remain? Surely admitting statistics, carrying logic and objectivity on the rising and plunging curves of their graphs like Vulcans on dolphin-back, better promotes the accuracy, rationality, and fairness of the fact-finding process than not admitting them.

### Why Rational Discrimination Is Not Reasonable

The most readily apparent objection to the reasonableness claim of the Bayesian challenges the statistical *method* he employs to assess the victim's dangerousness. Neither private nor judicial judgments about a particular member of a class, the argument goes, should rest on evidence about the class to which he or she belongs. Despite the attractiveness of this principle, and occasional court admonitions to avoid statistical inferences about individuals, private and judicial decision makers routinely rely on statistical evidence to judge past facts and predict future behavior. Lenders use statistics concerning age, marital status, location or residence, income, and assets to predict whether a borrower will repay a loan. Parole commissions may also use statistical techniques to predict parole success, considering factors such as number of prior convictions, type of crime, employment history, and family ties. And courts consider nonindividualized statistical probabilities when deciding whether to allow injured litigants to use epidemiological proof of causation in their lawsuits.

To accept the usefulness of statistical generalizations as a general matter, however, is *not* to agree that such generalizations are appropriate everywhere. For the use of statistical generalizations entail significant social costs, notwithstanding obvious benefits to defendants. The fatal flaw in the Bayesian's argument lies in his failure to take account of the costs of acting on

his racial generalizations. Instead, he assumes that the rationality of his factual judgments is all that matters in assessing the
reasonableness of his reactions. Thus, he asserts that if racial
identity incrementally increases the likelihood that an ambiguous Black man is about to attack (i.e., if it incrementally bolsters
the accuracy of his factual judgment that he is under attack),
then it is *reasonable* for him to use deadly force against the
Black more quickly than a similarly situated White. Whether a
reaction is *reasonable*, however, hinges not only on the rationality of its underlying factual judgments, but equally on the
consequences of error if those factual judgments are mistaken.

Consider one example of the injustices that lurk in the
Bayesian's lopsided attention to rationality. Ira Glasser of the
American Civil Liberties Union tells the story of a Black couple
who, some years ago, took in a movie in Times Square. It was
raining when they came out of the theater about 11 P.M., so the
husband went by himself for the car, which was parked in a
garage several blocks away. When he returned to pick up his
wife, she had disappeared. The man eventually discovered that
his wife, who was five months pregnant, had been arrested by
the police, put in jail, strip-searched and booked on charges of
loitering for the purpose of prostitution.

The arresting officer in this shocking incident may well have
viewed himself as an Intelligent Bayesian. Perhaps wrongly,
let's assume that at the time he made the arrest, there was a high
incidence of prostitution in Times Square, most of the prostitutes were unescorted women, a disproportionate number of
them were Black, and most transactions occurred between 10
P.M. and 2 A.M. The officer might assert that, from his standpoint, there was significant evidence to support his factual judgment that the woman was a prostitute—she was a woman,

Black, unescorted, and in Times Square at 11 o'clock at night. Even if we assume that his belief was rational in the sense that there was factual support for it, his *decision* to *act* on this belief in the way he did was patently *unreasonable*, not to mention outrageous and reprehensible. The reason his actions were unreasonable is because the costs of potential mistakes were so grievous. Given the enormous costs of potential mistakes, we rightly condemn him for not doing more to reduce the risk of being mistaken before subjecting this woman to such treatment. Many of us may express our concerns about the terrible costs of being wrong in this situation as doubt about whether the officer's factual judgments were rational. But, upon careful reflection, we see that we are really saying that given the potential for mistakes and the terrible consequences of his mistake, the actions of the officer were unreasonable, even if his factual judgment was rational in the sense that there were circumstances to support it.

To see this, consider two situations, in each of which I claim to know that my pet dog, a temperamental unpredictable Rottweiler, is chained to a tree in our fenced-in backyard. In the first case, I personally hook the chain to his collar three hours before bedtime. As I am turning in for the night, my wife asks me whether the dog is chained. If he really is still chained, he will simply spend the night in his doghouse as usual. But if he is not still chained, he will roam the backyard all night, strategically squirting urine on lawn chairs and fixtures in service of his territorial instincts. It takes fifteen minutes the following morning for me to retrace his steps and hose down all that he has marked—a chore I do not relish but cannot honestly characterize as more than an inconvenience. In such a case I would confidently claim to know the dog is chained and dive into bed.

In contrast, if my sister's one-year-old infant wanted to play in an area of our backyard beyond the reach of the chain and my sister asked me whether the dog is leashed, I would not claim to know that he is if I haven't checked on him in three hours. Put differently, it would not be *reasonable* for me to claim to know he is leashed in this situation. This is true even though the statistical risk of error in my factual judgment that the dog is leashed—that is, the *accuracy* of my factual judgment about the dog—is exactly the same in both situations. For the costs of error in the second case (the life of my niece) are infinitely greater than the costs of error in the first (momentary inconvenience). Thus, before claiming to know that he is leashed in the second case, I would gather more information to further reduce the risk of error by, for example, double-checking the chain and yanking on the collar several times. Holding the risk of error about the security of the leash constant in the two situations, my willingness to claim to know that the dog is secured varies according to the social consequences of error. Put differently, even if the rationality or accuracy of my factual judgment is the same in two situations, my willingness to claim to know something varies according to the social consequences of error.

The Bayesian tries to avoid discussion of the consequences of error by focusing solely on his subjective factual judgments, specifically, on whether his hastier conclusion that the "ambiguous" Black man was about to attack him was rational given that Blacks pose a marginally greater risk of assault than Whites. It is true that judging that one knows something may be a subjective thought process, a "state of mind." For example, when the officer, upon seeing the unescorted Black woman in Times Square in the late evening, concluded that she is a prostitute, something purely subjective occurred in his thought processes.

What the Bayesian overlooks, however, is that his hastier conclusion that he is under attack leads him to make a *decision* to *more hastily shoot* a Black man. The reasonableness of that *decision* and *act* (hastier use of deadly force against Blacks) is just as much at issue in these situations as the rationality of his hastier factual judgment that he was about to be attacked. To return to the Rottweiler example, to *claim* to know that something is the case is more than a thought process, it is a performance of a social *act*—it is to say something that lends assurance to others and which they will rely upon. In this respect a claim to knowledge is like a promise, another clearly social act. Thus, when I tell my wife as I hop into bed that I know the Rottweiler is leashed, I am assuring her that the risks of error in my factual judgment about the leash can be safely disregarded in view of the not-too-weighty interests (convenience) that a wrong judgment may injure. Likewise, when I tell my sister that I know the dog is leashed (which I do only after drastically reducing the risk of error by gathering more information on the condition of the leash), I am assuring her that the drastically reduced risks of error in my factual judgment are sufficiently small that they can be safely disregarded in view of the extremely weighty interests that a wrong judgment may injure.

   This same analysis applies to factual judgments and acts of the Bayesian. The Bayesian's hastier conclusion that an "ambiguous Black" is about to attack may be a subjective thought process—a subjective factual judgment. But when the Bayesian decides to act on his race-based factual judgment by using deadly force more quickly against ambiguous Blacks, he implies that the risks of error in his hastier use of deadly force against Blacks can be safely disregarded in view of the interests that wrong predictions will injure.

To determine whether the risks of error in race-based predictions about Blacks can be safely—that is, reasonably—disregarded, it is necessary to balance the *costs of waiting* for the "ambiguous" or "suspicious" Black to clarify his violent intentions against the *costs of not waiting*. For all predictions of human behavior present some risk of error. The more information we possess about a given situation, the smaller the risk of error in our judgments about it. Taking the time to gather information is costly, however. And nowhere are information costs higher than in self-defense cases, where the only way to gather more information is to wait for the "suspicious" person to manifest more clearly his violent intentions before responding with force. Here the *cost of waiting* translates into increased risk for the person who wants to defend herself successfully. If that person considers Blacks to pose a "significantly" greater threat of assault than Whites, she will not wait as long for an "ambiguous" Black person to clarify his violent intentions as for a White person.

On the other hand, the *costs of not waiting* as long for Blacks with unclear intentions as for similarly situated Whites include both the risks of error in race-based generalizations and the social consequences of error when the predictions prove false. First, consider the risks of error in race-based generalizations. Take the statistic for Black males arrested for violent assaults of approximately 2 percent (which is still much greater than the actual probability that a Black male will rob a stranger, since the violent assaults statistic also includes arrests for domestic violence, barroom brawls, street fights, heat of passion altercations between friends and acquaintances, turf wars between gang members, conflicts growing out of drug transactions, etc.), and assume this number represents the risk that the Black man entering the bank lobby in our hypothetical scenario was about to attack the woman at the ATM. Further assume that if this scenario occurred fifty different times to fifty different women throughout the city, in 2 percent of the cases—or one out of fifty times—the woman's belief that she was under attack was correct. This means that of the fifty Blacks against whom defenders use hastier lethal force because of racial generalizations, forty-nine will be innocent.

Next, consider the social consequences of error. The costs of error in race-based predictions of violence go well beyond the physical injuries suffered by the innocent Black victims of false predictions. Not waiting as long for Blacks to clarify their intentions has a profound "chilling effect" on Black participation in core community activities. That is, hastier use of force against Blacks forces Blacks who do not want to be mistaken for assailants to avoid ostensibly public places (such as "White" neighborhoods, automatic tellers, and even tony boutiques) and core community activities (such as shopping, jogging, sightseeing, or just "hanging out"). Further, Blacks who do venture into the public arena are compelled to stifle self-expression and move about in a withdrawn, timorous fashion lest they appear threatening to some anxious gun-toting pedestrian or subway rider.

An analogy may underscore the grim reality of "chilling effects." When I described the Times Square incident to a Black woman who teaches law at a major Midwestern university, she confided that she had also been mistaken for a prostitute on two occasions. On one, she had an appointment to meet someone at a hotel entrance. As she waited just outside the lobby door, a man in a business suit sidled up to her and asked what her services were going for. Ever since, she has strictly avoided meeting people at the entrance of hotels or in hotel lobbies, even though many law school conferences take place in hotels. On those occasions when she has no choice but to meet a group of people in a hotel lobby, she makes sure she arrives a little late so that she doesn't end up standing alone in the lobby before others arrive.

Another cost of not waiting concerns the denial of moral agency inflicted on Blacks by race-based suspicions. Race-based predictions of a person's behavior reduce him to a predictable object rather than treating him as a moral being capable of personal autonomy.[22] Of course, all predictions of human behavior undermine respect for personal autonomy to some degree. But respect for another's autonomy is especially undermined when the forecast that a person will choose to act violently is based on a factor—such as race—over which that person has no control.

Moreover, humiliation and stigmatization must be counted among the most painful costs of race-based suspicions. It is too easy for some to trivialize the severe psychological, emotional, and even spiritual costs to Blacks of being treated like criminals. For instance, according to Suzanna Sherry, a vocal critic of progressive feminist and minority perspectives on American justice, "[The] description of the young Black man who felt resentment when a White woman with a baby crossed the street to avoid him naturally invites a comparison: he fears for his emotional well-being, but she fears for her physical safety. *I, at least, would rather be snubbed than raped.*"[23] In saying that she would rather be "snubbed" than raped, Sherry speciously pits two certainties against each other—the certainty of being "snubbed" against the certainty of being raped. This is a gross distortion of the situation. In truth, the situation pits an extremely remote risk of being raped by a random Black man (nothing in the description of the situation suggested that the young man was acting in a threatening or erratic way) against the certainty of being "snubbed." Sherry's non sequitur vividly illustrates the rationality subverting power of stereotypes, for only by tapping the "Black as rapist" stereotype can she regard a rape by an ordinary Black man on an ordinary street *not* as an extremely remote risk but as a foregone conclusion.

More telling for "cost of not waiting" analysis is Sherry's trivialization of the humiliation and resentment suffered by the young Black man who was treated like a rapist. Characterizing the young man's injury as a case of being "snubbed" lumps it with breaches of social etiquette such as being ignored by an acquaintance or failing to receive an invitation to an ice cream social. The euphemism carries with it nothing of the relentless, cumulative, dehumanizing reality of these manifestations of the Black Tax par excellence. "Here we go again," muses the young Black man. "She's tripping all over herself to cross over to the other sidewalk, all the while cutting her eyes at me like I'm Willie Horton on work furlough. Somebody said being invisible was a terrible thing. I know something worse . . . being too visible . . . walking around with a screaming *BIG BLACK MAN* warning ineradicably tattooed across your forehead. They look right through invisible men, but the too-visible ones they use like movie screens for the projection of their most demeaning, pornographic images. I always feel like taking a bath after these encounters, but with so many to contend with everyday, if I tried to bathe after every one, I'd live in the bathtub." From the standpoint of doing justice to the severe dignitary injuries inflicted by these "microaggressions," a better comparison than "I'd rather be snubbed than raped" would be "I'd rather have waves of strangers successively spit in my face than run the extremely remote risk that a random anonymous Black man might rape me."

Once we consider the risks of error and the grave social consequences of error generated by statistical generalizations about race, we see that much more than number crunching is involved in assessing the reasonableness of using lethal force on the basis of such generalizations. Considerations of fairness and social justice figure as centrally in these assessments of reasonableness as considerations of factual accuracy. Telling defenders that they cannot base their decisions to shoot on racial generalizations may require them to wait slightly longer—as long as they would if the ambiguous person were White—than they would if they were allowed to use such generalizations. The costs of waiting (increased risk for defender) are not trivial. But when balanced against the costs of not waiting (injury or death to numerous innocent victims, exclusion of Blacks from core community activities, objectification, stigmatization, and humiliation), the scales of justice tilt decidedly in favor of the defender assuming the marginal additional risks of waiting.

Citizens are frequently called upon to incur additional risks for important principles and social values. Drafts for military service are obvious examples. Perhaps less obvious but much more pervasive are the health and safety risks we all incur in the interest of values such as freedom of expression, the right to bear arms, and even the less lofty values of technological progress (motor vehicles, for instance, take many more lives each year than they save, including many pedestrians)[24] and convenience (increases in the speed limit for cars exposes everyone on the highway to substantially greater danger, including those who continue to drive at the old lower speed limit).[25] We allow teenagers to drive, even though they generate an astonishingly disproportionate percentage of accidents, because we think it is important that they enjoy access to adult activities as part of their maturation process. Similarly, we license individuals with disabilities and prosthetic devices to drive, and hold them to a lower legal standard of reasonable care (in effect allowing them to generate more than ordinary risks without liability), because we believe it is important that they have equal access to core community activities. The list goes on, but this partial one suffices to show that expecting citizens to incur additional risks (especially additional risks as small as the ones being considered here) for the sake of important social interests is a familiar feature of our legal culture and social morality.

This analysis applies with equal force to shopkeepers, cabdrivers, and any other class of decision makers prone to screen "suspicious" persons on the basis of race. Shopkeepers and cabdrivers incur some risk in admitting "ambiguous" individuals. Yet, reducing Black Americans to second-class citizens by denying them equitable participation in social and commercial existence; subjecting the overwhelming majority of innocent Blacks to demeaning assumptions and microaggressions; contributing to the establishment of a de facto system of apartheid by private discriminatory decisions—these are the costs of race-based screening and they cannot be morally justified by the incremental risk. Sometimes, tragically, the risk of violent robbery, albeit small, is realized. By the same token, the risk of death or serious injury in automobiles and airplanes, albeit small, is realized hundreds of thousands of times every year. Yet we continue to expose ourselves to the risks of the airways and highways in ever-growing numbers. We simply do not live in a risk-free society, nor are we willing to sacrifice the values and conveniences that a dramatically less risky society would cost. Viewing our risk-laden social existence from this broader perspective, incremental race-based risks are not meaningfully different from thousands of other incremental risks we assume every day in return for a comfortable, convenient, decent, and democratic way of life. Accordingly, we must accept incremental race-based risks as the price of living in a just, humane, democratic society, as just, humane, democratic citizens.

In sum, the "Reasonable Person" does not discriminate against Blacks on the basis of racial generalizations. The Reasonable Person can be fairly expected to surmount his or her discriminatory impulses and incur incremental race-based risks to protect vital democratic values. Because the reasonable and the moral are flip sides of the same coin,[26] an individual who shoots or screens others on racial grounds engages in blameworthy conduct. Bluntly put, the Bayesian's decision to discriminate against Blacks on the basis of statistical generalizations is racist.

Some readers may recoil at the use of the value-laden term "racist" to describe ostensibly rational racial discrimination. As we have seen, however, assessments of reasonableness essentially turn on a balancing of values, making the term "reasonable" itself a value-laden expression. Referring to the Bayesian's discriminatory decisions as racist simply stresses that they strike an unreasonable balance in a way that wrongfully devalues or undervalues the democratic interests of Black Americans in being treated as full and equal citizens.

Saying that so-called rational discrimination is racist is not the same as saying that all cabdrivers, shopkeepers, and others who have historically discriminated against Blacks on grounds they believed to be rational are incorrigible racists. Many well-intentioned people simply have not had the enormous costs and incremental gains of their discriminatory decisions put in perspective. The racist is the person who says, "Yes, I appreciate the large risks of error and the grave social consequences of error that racial generalizations involve. And, yes, I understand that everyday I willingly expose myself to many risks greater than those incremental risks posed by Blacks, in some cases for lofty reasons and in other cases for very mundane ones. Nevertheless, I do not consider the interests of Black Americans worth incurring any incremental risks for. So I will not buzz them in, pick them up, or wait as long to shoot an 'ambiguous' one as I would wait for a similarly situated White." Appeals to principle like those developed in this discussion may reach only those well-intentioned people who seek to avoid racism, and who therefore can be persuaded to stop engaging in racist practices. Racially illiberal Americans who refuse to adequately credit the interests of Blacks in their decision making, on the other hand, require alternative approaches to helping them avoid discrimination. We will discuss some alternative approaches for racially illiberal decision makers in the last chapter.

This analysis retains its vitality even if the risk estimates concerning Black assaults are modified. There may continue to be debate about the most accurate risk-of-assault statistics for Blacks, but as long as the risks of error in the racial generalizations remain high, and the social consequences of error remain grave and far-reaching, moral and policy arguments against using statistical generalizations to visit serious injuries on Blacks remain compelling.

### Race and the Subversion of Rationality

The preceding discussion assumed that considering race might incrementally promote rationality by marginally increasing the accuracy of factual judgments of risk, but concluded that the benefits of these incremental gains in rationality are so decisively outweighed by the social and moral costs of race-based predictions that relying on race is unreasonable. Now we examine how considering race in self-defense cases can undermine rationality itself. However pure a defender's conscious intentions, considering the race of an "ambiguous" Black person before shooting him impairs the capacity of the defender rationally and fairly to strike a balance between the costs of waiting and the costs of not waiting. By the same token, permitting a defendant who shoots a "suspicious" Black person to focus on race at trial, even for the ostensibly neutral purpose of supporting the rationality of his factual judgments, impairs the capacity of jurors rationally and fairly to strike the same balance.

A large and compelling body of social science research—including case studies, studies of conviction rates, death penalty statistics, laboratory findings in mock jury studies, and general research on racial prejudice—establishes that racial bias affects jury deliberations.[27] These studies indicate two distinct kinds of jury bias operating in criminal cases: own-race favoritism and other-race antagonism. Both kinds of bias subvert the rationality of the decisionmaking process in self-defense cases.

Other-race antagonism tends to cause White decision makers to devalue the interests of the Black victim and the group to which he belongs. The tendency of juries to devalue the lives of Blacks can be seen in the proven tendency of juries to punish defendants more severely when their victims are White than when they are Black, suggesting that the lives of minority victims are valued less highly than White victims.[28] Conversely, own-race favoritism tends to cause White decision makers to overvalue the interests of the White defender and the group to which he belongs.[29] In other words, through racially selective sympathy and indifference, decision makers (often unconsciously) fail to feel as much sympathy and exercise as much care for marginalized people as they routinely do for their own group. Consequently, they tend to misassess the comparative costs and benefits of their decisions for the respective groups.

In self-defense cases, this means that conscious or unconscious bias may cause both defenders and juries (often all White)[30] to miscalculate the costs of not waiting as long for Blacks to reveal their intentions as for non-Blacks, since an individual and a group with which they do not identify will bear those costs, while "one of their own" would bear the cost of waiting for a suspected assailant to exhibit his violent intentions.[31] Thus, even if the racial factor marginally promotes rationality on the issue of risk assessment, it substantially undermines the rational determination of how long the defender should have waited for the stranger to clarify his intentions before resorting to deadly force. In the professional patois of lawyers and judges, its "probative value [may be] substantially outweighed by the danger of unfair prejudice." And surely a paragon of rational thinking like the "Intelligent Bayesian" would not urge us improperly to fasten upon a factor that subverts the rationality of the fact-finding process.[32]

Fortunately, and seemingly paradoxically, there is a way for decision makers properly to focus on the racial factor. Unlike the Bayesian, who considers race to justify his quicker use of force against "ambiguous" Blacks, decision makers can approach race-consciousness in a way that helps them avoid giving in to their discriminatory impulses to treat Blacks (and other marginalized groups) less favorably than Whites. Rationality-enhancing color-consciousness is examined in the last chapter.

# Chapter Three

# THE "INVOLUNTARY NEGROPHOBE"

Among the many violent reactions I had in the weeks following the rape, including despair, helplessness, a sense that
my life was over, was a visceral, desperate fear of all strange
Black and brown men. Walking alone in Mount Pleasant, an
inner-city Washington, D.C., neighborhood, I had a panic
attack as it seemed that each of the dozens of Central American men streaming toward and past me on the sidewalk was
about to pull a knife and stab me.[1]

This frank and chilling description by Micaela di Leonardo, a
former rape crisis counselor, of her reaction to being raped by a
Black male suggests the profoundly personal level on which the
link between race and violence may be forged. In contrast to
both the "Reasonable Racist" (whose fear of Blacks stems from
and is reinforced by the mass media and traditional racial

myths) and the "Intelligent Bayesian" (whose racial fears rest on crime statistics), di Leonardo's fear emerged after a violent personal assault. To what extent, then, should such "involuntary Negrophobia" be relevant to claims of self-defense?

Suppose the patron who shot the young Black man in our ATM scenario had been brutally mugged by Black teenagers nine months before the night of the shooting. Suppose further that after the mugging she developed what her psychiatrist diagnosed as a posttraumatic stress disorder, triggered by contact with Blacks, which induced her to overestimate the Black victim's threat on the night of the shooting. Under these circumstances, the defendant could claim that her admittedly paranoid fear of the young Black victim was "reasonable" for someone mugged in the past by Black assailants.

As open-ended and dangerous as this claim of reasonableness may seem, the legal system has already accepted its underlying doctrinal and psychological propositions. The doctrinal foundation of the Negrophobe's claim is the widely accepted "subjective" test of reasonableness, which makes allowances for the psychological effects of the defendant's past experiences.[2] Under this standard of reasonableness, as long as a "typical" person who suffered the same traumatic experiences as the defendant could develop the same misperceptions, the defendant's misperceptions will be found reasonable. For example, a battered woman who kills her abusive partner in a "nonconfrontational" situation (during a lull in the violence or when the abuser was asleep) must convince the fact finder that, at the time she killed her partner, she reasonably believed that she needed to act imminently to protect herself from serious injury or death.[3] In proving her case, the battered woman defendant may concede that battered woman syndrome—a subcategory of posttraumatic stress disorder—caused her to overestimate the sleeping man's dangerousness and to underestimate her capacity to escape the battering relationship. She may nonetheless contend that she acted reasonably on the ground that a reasonable person *in her situation* would have perceived the threat in the same way.

The psychological premise underlying the Negrophobe's claim is that a typical person assaulted by a Black individual could conceivably develop a pathological phobia toward *all* Blacks. Surprisingly, in a recent Florida case,[4] a judge awarded workers' compensation benefits to a Negrophobic claimant on precisely this basis. Even more surprisingly, every appellate court that reviewed this controversial case affirmed the benefits award.[5]

In the Florida case, Ruth Jandrucko, a fifty-nine-year-old White woman, filed a workers' compensation claim after she was mugged by a young Black male while making a customer service visit for her employer.[6] As a result of the attack, she suffered a fractured vertebra in her back and developed what experts diagnosed as a posttraumatic stress disorder causing physical and psychological reactions to Blacks.[7] Although her vertebral fracture eventually healed, her phobia toward Blacks—particularly "big, Black males"—persisted.[8] Ms. Jandrucko claimed that her phobia rendered her incapable of working around African Americans; hence, she argued, she could not find gainful employment.[9]

Accepting Ms. Jandrucko's argument, Florida compensation claims Judge John G. Tomlinson, Jr., awarded her total disability benefits for her phobia.[10] In reaching his decision, Judge Tomlinson found that before her assault Ms. Jandrucko exhibited no apparent "pre-existing racial prejudice or predisposition to psychiatric illness."[11] In other words, she was an ordinary person before the assault. As reported in the *Washington Post,* Judge Tomlinson commented that Ms. Jandrucko's pathological fear of Blacks was not an exercise of "'private racial prejudice,'" but instead a mere "work-related phobia."[12] In Judge Tomlinson's view, "It is not relevant what the subject of her phobia is."[13]

### The Involuntary Negrophobe and Dueling Conceptions of Law

Judge Tomlinson's statement illustrates one side of the ongoing debate between instrumentalist and noninstrumentalist conceptions of law. The noninstrumentalist approach focuses exclusively on the personal culpability of the individual defendant, without regard for any social implications beyond the boundaries of the immediate case. Noninstrumentalists argue that legal liability should be imposed solely to redress a specific wrong between the particular parties to a particular dispute, not to send messages to society or promote social policies.[14] In short, this approach focuses on specific parties and the past.

From the standpoint of personal culpability, the sine qua non of criminal liability for noninstrumentalists, Judge Tomlinson may seem to have rightly concluded that the subject of a person's pathological phobia is not relevant. This view emphasizes the involuntary nature of a posttraumatic stress disorder: insofar as a defendant can claim that "I couldn't help myself," she cannot be blamed for her reactions, regardless of the subject of her disorder.[15] Thus, under a purely noninstrumental regime, there may seem to be no reason to limit legal recognition of Negrophobia to workers' compensation cases; once an involuntary condition is identified in any context, no just basis exists for imposing legal liability on an actor.[16]

Of course, a person who cannot control her reactions to Blacks may be blameworthy for taking a loaded gun to a public place where she might encounter Blacks; but then her earlier decision to put herself in such a position would be blameworthy, not the involuntary reaction itself. We shall assume that a jury could find it reasonable for a person suffering from Negrophobia to carry a loaded weapon on a brief excursion from her home. That a jury could find such behavior reasonable would not shock me, given the outlandish police conduct the Simi Valley jury found reasonable in the first Rodney King case. Judgments of reasonableness can turn significantly on jurors' identification with a defendant and lack of identification with a victim.[17]

The instrumentalist approach, in contrast, focuses on the broader implications of recognizing some legal claims and withholding legal recognition from others.[18] Instrumentalism refers to legal decision making that considers the social implications of legal rules and aims to affect future behavior. Instrumentalists view the law as an instrument of social change and public policy, and they see nothing wrong with employing legal rules as carrots and sticks, to encourage and deter persons other than the immediate parties to the dispute, nor with framing rules to send important social messages. Promoting the general welfare by refusing to recognize legal claims that damage the integrity of the legal system is one example of an instrumentalist approach to legal decision making.

Legal recognition of the Involuntary Negrophobe's claims would subvert the general welfare by destroying the legitimacy of the courts. The paramount social function of the courts is the resolution of disputes. But the power of a third party to conclusively resolve disputes must rest on some basis, such as his priestly authority, his charisma, or his reputation for Solomonic wisdom in the administration of justice.[19] In a complex, impersonal, and officially secular society like ours, this basis is the courts' apparent objectivity, particularly their neutrality with respect to the parties before them.[20] The widespread sense of injustice that followed the acquittal of four police officers in the Rodney King beating case, triggering some of the worst rioting in American history, reveals a tangible price that society pays when courts lose their perceived objectivity, and thus their legitimacy, in the eyes of at least some in society. Significantly, the riots did not erupt when the images of King's beating initially saturated the airwaves, but only after the announcement of the verdicts. The Black and Latino communities waited for the justice system to honor its promise of neutrality, and many of their members took to the streets only when that promise seemed so blatantly flouted.

Were courts to sanction the contention that a person's racial fear was so overwhelming that it constitutes an excuse for violence against Blacks, they would have to equate severe racial fear with recognized judgment-impairing conditions—such as insanity and youthfulness—which, when successfully invoked, justify a "not guilty determination."[21] Treating "Negrophobia" like insanity, however, raises additional legitimacy problems. Despite the general acknowledgment that genuine insanity may so severely impair an individual's sense of reality, of right, and of wrong as to nullify the possibility of culpability for that individual, there is a widespread perception that sane but guilty defendants exploit the insanity defense to escape long mandatory prison sentences or the death penalty.[22] Were people to develop the same skepticism with respect to defenses invoking Negrophobia, the result might well be a total loss of faith in the criminal justice system's ability to adjudicate race-based claims fairly and effectively. Blacks, already concerned with a perceived dual standard operating in the court system,[23] would justifiably perceive the courts' crediting of such claims as the advent of a new legal loophole potentially enabling racists to express their venomous prejudices without consequence.

Of course, when a defendant is declared not guilty by reason of insanity, he is not excused "without consequence." Legally insane defendants are often sent to institutions for long periods of time. But a defendant pleading Negrophobia would be claiming to suffer a posttraumatic stress disorder, not insanity. As with battered woman syndrome, posttraumatic stress disorders support excuses that, when accepted, shield the defendant from any further legal consequences. Thus, there would be even more substantial grounds for skepticism about defenses invoking Negrophobia than defenses invoking insanity.

# Chapter Four

# OF MICE AND MEN:
# EQUAL PROTECTION AND
# UNCONSCIOUS BIAS

The United States Constitution. For some, when all other pleas for racial fairness fall on deaf or indifferent ears, hope can still find something to reach for in the United States Constitution, once thought to be the surest handhold on the precipitous cliff of American racial justice. Faith in the ability of the Constitution to promote racial justice has been flagging in recent years, however. Each new term brings fresh news of retrenchment in constitutional protections for marginalized groups. Fortunately, however, reports of the death of constitutional guarantees for historically oppressed peoples have been greatly exaggerated. Whether the Reasonable Racist, Intelligent Bayesian, and Involuntary Negrophobe pass constitutional muster, therefore, remains a vital issue.

Constitutional doctrine is in a state of turbulence, roiling beneath the vicissitudes of party politics and political appointments. A lengthy analysis of current constitutional doctrine, therefore, might be dated before the ink dries. Whatever ends constitutional doctrine seeks to serve, however, it cannot serve those ends if it is steeped in faulty assumptions about the way the world works, especially the workings of the human mind.

### Private Bias and Equal Protection

Courts have long invoked the Equal Protection Clause of the Fourteenth Amendment, which prohibits the states from denying any person the equal protection of the laws,[1] to invalidate racially discriminatory laws, and to prohibit racially discriminatory state action.[2] In the most straightforward case, when a state explicitly classifies a group of people by race, the classification is "suspect" and subject to "strict scrutiny" under the Equal Protection Clause.[3] Under strict scrutiny, a racial classification is constitutionally valid only if it is necessary to further a "compelling" state interest.[4]

*Palmore v. Sidoti*[5] is a leading case illustrating the application of strict scrutiny doctrine to evaluate a race-based claim of equal protection. In *Palmore*, a Florida court in 1980 granted custody of a three-year-old girl to her White mother upon her parents' divorce. The following year, the father sought custody of the child by petitioning to modify the prior judgment on the basis of changed conditions, including the fact that his former wife was living with, and subsequently married, a Black man, Clarence Palmore, Jr. Even though the Florida court admittedly had no reason to doubt the mother's devotion to her daughter, the adequacy of housing facilities, or the respectability of her new spouse, it ordered custody of the child transferred to her father. The primary rationale for the court's order was that the child would suffer social stigmatization if she remained in an interracial household with her mother.

Applying strict scrutiny, the Supreme Court found that the Florida court's order to transfer custody violated the Equal Protection Clause. In reversing the judgment, the Supreme Court noted the persistence of racial prejudice in America, acknowledging the "risk that a child living with a stepparent of a different race may be subject to a variety of pressures and stresses not present if the child were living with parents of the same racial or ethnic origin."[6] Nevertheless, in a unanimous and strongly worded opinion, the Court held that "[t]he effects of racial prejudice, *however real*, cannot justify a racial classification removing an infant child from the custody of its natural mother."[7] While recognizing that "private biases may be outside the reach of the law," the Court stressed that "the law cannot, *directly or indirectly, give [these biases] effect.*"[8] The Court's unusual interference with a state custody decision in *Palmore*, including its determination that the state's parens patriae interest in the welfare of children was not compelling, reveal the strength of its resolve to prohibit the use of racial classifications that give effect to private bias in courts of law.

Someone representing the interests of a Black person who was shot by a race-conscious defender could seek to keep the defendant from raising race-based defenses by arguing that such defenses violate the equal protection clause. To advance the equal protection argument under *Palmore*, one must first clear two more technical hurdles—namely, the litigant must demonstrate the requisite state action[9] and the existence of a racially restrictive category[10]—and then he or she must prove that enforcement of the category (i.e., permitting the race-conscious defendant to assert his race-based defense) would "give effect to private bias." Private bias does not always advertise its existence, however. We must sometimes reach beyond the obvious to root it out.

### THE REASONABLE RACIST

The Reasonable Racist presents the simplest case. In arguing that he should be exonerated on the ground that racist responses are typical—and thus reasonable—the Reasonable Racist openly admits his racial bias. Thus, to hear the Reasonable Racist's claim, the judge would have to employ a racial classification that gives effect to racial bias. Under *Palmore*, a judge who employs such a classification—even for a very good reason—infringes the Equal Protection Clause of the Fourteenth Amendment.

### THE INTELLIGENT BAYESIAN

Unlike the Reasonable Racist, the Intelligent Bayesian does not admit to personal bias. Since he claims that his racial fears rest on a valid factual basis, he may contend that a court that permits him to stress or merely discretely allude to the racial factor in proving his reasonableness would not be employing an impermissible racial classification that "gives effect to private bias" in violation of *Palmore*.

We can reject this argument under either of two rationales. First, we can question the Bayesian's objectivity in selectively rejecting or ignoring evidence that conflicts with a cultural stereotype. Recall the studies showing that once an individual internalizes a tacitly transmitted cultural stereotype, he unconsciously interprets experiences to be consistent with the underlying stereotype, selectively assimilating facts that validate the stereotype while disregarding those that do not.[11] To the extent that the Bayesian aggressively assimilates negative statistical information about Blacks, while remaining oblivious to contradictory or positive statistical information, he undermines his claim of objectivity. Countenancing the Bayesian's argument under these circumstances would give effect to private bias.

Second, even conceding the possibility of a genuinely bias-free Bayesian, allowing him to emphasize the racial factor would give effect to racial bias in the jury box. Recall that there is compelling empirical evidence that racial bias routinely infects jury deliberations, suggesting that the men and women charged with evaluating the reasonableness of the defendant's actions are anything but bias-free Bayesians. Although the racial identity of the Black victim will inevitably become clear in the course of the trial, playing on this factor may exacerbate the (often unconscious) bias that it taps in a White jury.

### THE INVOLUNTARY NEGROPHOBE

At first blush, the claim of the Negrophobe may seem an easy case in view of *Palmore*, for a phobia about Blacks may be a paradigmatic expression of private bias. The Negrophobe, however, may convincingly disclaim having consciously harbored any racist sentiments before the assault that induced her disorder. In fact, the hallmark of the Involuntary Negrophobe's self-characterization is the absence of racial animus prior to the catalyzing incident. The judge presiding over the Ruth Jandrucko hearing, for example, ruled that Ms. Jandrucko showed no apparent racial prejudice before her assault and hence was not exercising a "private racial prejudice" in her pathological paranoia of Blacks. The racial factor, contends the Negrophobe, is merely coincidental. It is something her psyche randomly seized upon and involuntarily associates with the trauma of the earlier assault.

But the characterization of the Negrophobe's pathological paranoia as a case of involuntary bias may be too glib. Recall the "visceral, desperate fear of all strange Black and brown men" that Professor di Leonardo felt in the weeks following her rape by a Black man. These emotions apparently did not stem from any conscious racial animus: di Leonardo recounts that after her rape she "ended up, with no small sense of irony, lecturing cops, co-workers, relatives, and friends alike" on the falsity of the stereotype about black men and interracial rape.[12] Yet, in spite of her unflagging personal and professional commitment to the fight against racial prejudice, she developed an uncontrollable fear not, significantly, of all strange men, but of "all strange black and brown men."[13] Thus, at the same time that we accept the Negrophobe's claim that she was not *consciously* biased before the catalyzing event, we may wonder whether *unconscious* bias fueled the peculiar phobia developed after the event.

The problem with the Negrophobe's argument is its suggestion that "private bias" must manifest *self-conscious* racial prejudice to be unconstitutional. This approach rests on an impoverished understanding of the nature of the evil—invidious racial discrimination—that the Equal Protection Clause seeks to eradicate.

*Beyond "conscious bias."* A key insight of modern psychology is that our minds are often not conscious of what directs them. Especially stereotypes, as I show in chapter 6, operate largely in the realm of the unconscious. Accordingly, to successfully eliminate governmental action that gives effect to racial bias, equal protection doctrine must accommodate the increasingly incontrovertible insights of modern psychology into unconscious discrimination.

We need only consider how often we act on unconsidered assumptions about the world to understand the prevalence of unconscious motivation. A student who traverses a hallway between two classrooms while intently perusing the sports page of her hometown newspaper "assumes" that the floor will be there to receive each successive footfall. Her failure to forsake the box scores for an unobstructed view of the familiar floor beneath her is deeply rooted in this assumption, and the possibility that the floor might not be there does not "occur" to her, that is, is not present in her conscious mental processes. Assumptions of this kind, called "tacit assumptions," are psychological states that shape and direct an individual's behavior without being present in her consciousness.[14]

Especially instructive insight regarding the operation of tacit assumptions comes from experiments roughly measuring the relative strength of an animal's "assumptions":

> If a rat is trained for months to run through a particular maze, the sudden interposition of a barrier in one of the channels will have a very disruptive effect on its behavior. For some time after encountering the barrier, it will be likely to engage in random and apparently pointless behavior, running in circles, scratching itself, etc. The degree to which the barrier operates disruptively reflects the strength of the "assumption" made by the rat that it would not be there. If the maze has been frequently changed, and the rat has only recently become accustomed to its present form, the introduction of a barrier will act less disruptively. In such a case, after a relatively short period of random behavior, the rat will begin to act purposively, will retrace its steps, seek other outlets, etc. In this situation the "assumption" that the channel would not be obstructed has not been deeply etched into the

rat's nervous system; it behaves as if it "half-expected" some such impediment.[15]

In the terms of the maze analogy, racial stereotypes are channels laid out by our cultural belief system. We first traverse these culturally embedded channels in response to either explicit lessons or "tacit understandings."[16] Tacit understandings instill stereotypes in ways that escape conscious detection, causing us to traverse the channels largely unconsciously. For instance, although local and national news anchors do not openly announce that Blacks are "prone to violence" on the nightly news, the relentless and selective representation of Black violence in the mass media tacitly transmits the same message. Because stereotypes saturate our society, and because our culture often rewards individuals for exaggerating the differences between themselves and members of other racial groups,[17] we travel these channels repeatedly. If an individual has never known a Black professional or has a mental medley of Black images primarily composed of the comedian, criminal, musician, or athlete stereotypes, no unexpected barriers have materialized to force a detour in his development of negative attitudes toward Blacks. Moreover, even if this individual encounters Blacks who do not conform to the cultural stereotype, he will often reject or ignore such counterevidence rather than retrace his steps to explore other ways of thinking about Blacks.[18] In time, these stereotypes become deeply etched in the individual's psyche, conditioning and directing his behavior without his awareness. (Chapter 6 gives a detailed account of the cognitive underpinnings of unconscious bias.)

*The relationship between unconscious bias and assault-induced Negrophobia.* Once we recognize that racially discriminatory

behavior is directly and inevitably rooted in unconscious discrimination fostered by our society's tacit assumptions and
biases, the rationale for denying the Negrophobe's claim
becomes clear. Regardless of how racially liberal Ms. Jandrucko,
Professor di Leonardo, and our hypothetical Negrophobe consciously believe themselves to have been before their respective
assaults, they undoubtedly harbored some unconscious bias that
ripened into Negrophobia after the assaults. Virtually every
person in our society consciously or unconsciously compiles a
mental library of Black stereotypes over the course of his or her
life. The belief that Blacks are prone to commit violent assaults
is among the most powerful and frightening myths in this
library. Consequently, being assaulted by a Black person cannot
help but resonate with preexisting stereotypes in profound and
unpredictable ways. The resonance may vary in intensity and
duration, ranging from a mild and ephemeral hypersensitivity
to a severe and lasting phobia. But whatever the magnitude of
this resonance in any particular case, the possibility of any race-
based reaction at all depends entirely on the preexistence of
racial bias, conscious or unconscious.

An alternative explanation for the Negrophobe's assault-
induced fear of all Blacks essentially asserts that the Negrophobe
"just happens" to strongly associate one of the assailant's prominent traits (skin color) with the attack. According to this argument, any one of the assailant's physical traits—his hair color,
height, or facial hair, for instance—is equally likely to precipitate
a phobic response in a victim. Thus, the Negrophobe's response
stems not from racial bias, but from an arbitrary linkage in her
subconscious between the assault and the attacker's skin color.

Were race-based phobias the products of random and nondis-
criminatory mental connections, we would expect a wide range of

physical characteristics to trigger hypersensitivities or pathological fears in assault victims. Hypersensitivity to hair color, for
instance, should be at least as common among assault victims as
Negrophobia. But the reason victims do not link their assailants'
hair color to violence with anything resembling the patterned reg-
ularity with which they link race to violence is that in our culture
hair color—but not race—is strictly a matter of superficial physiology. Eye color, too, is viewed as a superficial and easily over-
looked characteristic. (In a popular Elton John release from the
1970s, the singer croons of his lover's eyes, "excuse me forgetting,
but these things I do / You see I've forgotten if they're green or
they're blue . . .") Like hair and eye color, skin color would signify
nothing beyond superficial appearances in a culture that did not
attach the peculiar significance to the social construct "race" that
ours does. It is precisely because we do attach (irrationally and
often unconsciously) such significance to "race" that Negrophobic assault victims forge lasting psychological links between a single violent encounter and the "race" of their assailant.

Because much of the bias that drives race-based discrimination is unconscious, the Equal Protection Clause must reach such
bias if it is to serve its protective function. Since assault-induced
phobias of Blacks rests on conscious or unconscious bias, admitting evidence of such a phobia, even if the defendant claims it is
involuntary, employs an explicit racial classification and gives
effect to racial bias in violation of the Equal Protection Clause.

### Restructuring the Maze to Serve Justice

The fault line running between instrumentalism and nonin-
strumentalism, the leitmotif of the last chapter, figures centrally
here, too. The foregoing equal protection arguments, perhaps

especially those of the Negrophobe, undoubtedly strike noninstrumentalists as irrelevant in view of their conviction that punishing individuals for psychological conditions beyond their control—or knowledge—is unjust. This is the "just deserts" school of criminal justice. From this perspective, punishment is just only if measured by the desert of the offender, and the desert of an offender is gauged by his character—that is, the kind of person he is. In the self-defense context, where a defendant's mistaken or premature use of deadly force is attributable to a posttraumatic stress disorder, her act does not indicate what kind of person she is. Therefore, concludes the noninstrumentalist, it is unfair to punish the Negrophobe in this situation.

This argument, however, ignores the historical application of the Equal Protection Clause along instrumentalist lines. One central and long-standing concern of the courts applying the Equal Protection Clause has been the elimination of racial stigmatization.[19] The essence of stigma is being forced to wear a badge or symbol that degrades the stigmatized person *in the eyes of society*.[20] Because stigmatizing actions injure by virtue of the meaning society gives them, courts must weigh the social implications of legal doctrines in judging whether they infringe on protections guaranteed by the Equal Protection Clause. The courts' application of equal protection doctrine to eradicate racially stigmatizing practices, therefore, necessarily involves an instrumentalist assessment of the social consequences of adopting certain legal rules.

In the case of the panic-stricken bank patron, granting legal recognition to her self-defense claim communicates the state's approval of racial bias regardless of what theory she pursues; it sends the message that "your dread of Blacks is a valid excuse for taking the life of an innocent Black person." In conveying such messages, the court reinforces derogatory cultural stereotypes and stigmatizes all Americans of African descent.

The antithesis between instrumental and noninstrumental conceptions of the law stems from a deeper antinomy between two paramount functions of the law with respect to human behavior—the responsive function and the channeling function. In its responsive function, the law merely responds to the behavior of ordinary people by adjusting its rules to their beliefs, attitudes, and assumptions, including their "tacit assumptions." In its channeling function, the law proactively disciplines behavior and guides it into proper channels. (This distinction precisely parallels the one between "observing" and "defining" the reasonable man standard discussed at the end of chapter 2.) To return to the maze analogy, the law cannot merely be concerned with adjusting its rules to fit a cultural belief system that induces individuals to repeatedly traverse stereotypical channels (and make some of us susceptible to pathological phobias). The law must also strive to lay out the channels of the maze, and to eliminate those pathways that foster the oppression of minorities. It must weigh the costs and benefits of conforming to prevailing assumptions against the costs and benefits of reshaping those assumptions.[21]

Under the noninstrumental model, the law must take the human animal as he is conditioned and simply ask whether society can fairly expect individuals to overcome their conditioning under the circumstances. According to the instrumentalist view, the law should seek to alter the maze and retrain individuals by formulating rules that prevent the stigmatization of Blacks, reflect the community's moral aspirations of racial equality, and help eradicate racial discrimination.

The dilemma posed by the Reasonable Racist, the Intelligent

Bayesian, and the Involuntary Negrophobe stems directly from the law's roots in both instrumentalist and noninstrumentalist conceptions of legal liability, and from the justice system's effort both to accommodate the behavior of ordinary persons and to encourage desirable behavior. The dilemma does not lend itself to facile solutions; we must submit ourselves to one or the other of its horns. In this case, the least destructive horn is the one that refuses to give the state's imprimatur to racial bias—whether conscious or unconscious, voluntary or involuntary.

# Chapter Five

# BLAME AND PUNISHMENT: NARRATIVE, PERSPECTIVE, SCAPE-GOATS, AND DEMONS

Narrative has never been merely entertainment for me. It is, I believe, one of the principal ways in which we absorb knowledge.

—Toni Morrison, *The Nobel Lecture in Literature*, 1993

Storytelling—narrative—shapes our responses to the world. It excites and channels our passions and sympathies, inviting us to become certain kinds of people (compassionate and understanding or self-righteous and vindictive, for example) to the extent that we give ourselves over to its point of view. Narrative, moreover, can be subversive. What is taken for granted in a dominant narrative—truth, common sense, reasonableness—may be fiercely contested in the outsider version.

The framing of narrative, therefore, carries profoundly political implications. Put differently, the terms of narrative are prizes in a pitched conflict among groups attempting to describe their social reality, constitute their social identity, and vindicate their social existence. Understanding the stakes of narrative in this way underscores the vital importance of battered women's self-defense work and explains much of the stubborn resistance to this work.[1] For as much as anything, criminal trials (which, like all trials, consist of highly ritualized and formalized storytelling) are battles over the terms of narrative.

Two of the fundamental elements of any narrative are context and perspective—how much of the story gets told and from whose point of view. Knowing the truth of the old legal adage that "he who frames the issue wins on the merits," each party to a legal dispute seeks to frame the dispute's context and perspective to his or her own advantage. The state in criminal cases typically seeks to frame context and perspective narrowly, so that the focus is limited to the isolated criminal incident, and so that the perspective from which the incident is viewed is limited to that of the dominant race, class, and gender. To this end, the state employs three methodological devices. First, it seeks a narrow time frame that excludes evidence about events leading up to the criminal incident.[2] Second, it seeks to exclude evidence about the social, cultural, and economic conditions surrounding that incident.[3] Third, it seeks to define the reasonable person standard— the standard that tells the fact finders whose perspective they should adopt in assessing the facts—so that the defendant's personal history and attributes are rendered irrelevant.[4]

Conversely, defendants often want the fact finder to evaluate the criminal incident within a broad time frame; in view of its broader social, cultural, and economic realities; and from the perspective of someone like the defendant. Generally, traditional criminal law has sided with the state by dictating that courts narrowly frame context and adopt the dominant perspective. Nevertheless, despite stubborn resistance from traditional legal thinkers and some courts, advocates for battered women have succeeded in helping their clients frame their narratives broadly enough to do justice to the fullness of their circumstances and experiences. Battered women who kill their abusive partner in "nonconfrontational" situations (during a lull in the violence or while the abuser was asleep) have posed special challenges for advocates.[5]

## Framing the Narrative Broadly in Women's Self-Defense Work

Advocates for battered women challenge the restrictions on narrative inscribed in traditional criminal law in two crucial respects. First, advocates press traditional criminal law to depart from its dominant tendency to focus narrowly on the criminal incident.[6] Specifically, women's self-defense work urges traditional criminal law to broaden its time frame to take account of earlier events leading up to the criminal incident, such as the abuser's history of threats and physical abuse, the escalation in violence over time, and the woman's efforts to reduce her and her children's exposure to further violence. Moreover, women's self-defense work presses criminal law doctrine to consider the situational obstacles to a woman leaving a battering relationship, such as economic necessity; the frequent inability of police, restraining orders, and even shelters to protect battered women; and the high incidence of separation assault in which efforts to leave trigger more severe or lethal reactions by abusers.[7]

Second, activists for battered women stress the importance of assessing the woman's decisions and actions from the perspective of someone in her position. It urges that the battered woman's conduct be judged against an individualized standard of reasonableness in which the jurors ask themselves whether an ordinary person "in the shoes of the defendant" could have reacted as she did. The so-called objective test of reasonableness, which courts sometimes tell fact finders to employ in evaluating the defendant's reactions, directs the fact finders to assess the defendant's situation from the perspective of an average person drawn from the general population. The "objective" test, therefore, is a bed of Procrustes that directs fact finders to *ignore* the special attributes of the defendant—such as a posttraumatic stress disorder or an enhanced capacity to predict the behavior of her partner—which she developed from her history of abuse.

### Narrative, Consent, and Blame

Traditional legal scholars and conservative courts oppose defendants' efforts to broaden and individualize their narratives because they fear the potential impact of such considerations on our ability to treat the defendant's "choice" to violate the law as truly "free." For traditional scholars must posit "free choice" to get their justifications of criminal punishment off the ground. To punish a person, according to these theorists, we must first determine that he or she is blameworthy. Normally, we can infer a blameworthy character from a decision by the actor to break the law. But the inference from bad act to bad character only holds if the defendant's decision or choice to break the law was free. If the defendant's choice was determined by external forces, that choice does not tell us what kind of person he or she is. Thus, "[I]f a bank teller opens a safe and turns money over to a stranger, we can [normally] infer that he is dishonest. But if he does all this at gunpoint, we cannot infer anything one way or the other about his honesty."[8] And if we do not know what kind of person he is, we cannot blame him. Before we can condemn, therefore, we must conclude that the defendant's choices were free.

Once we see how the dominant theory of blame and punishment hinges on free choice, we also see why setting and perspective are so hotly contested in criminal trials. The more we ignore the events leading up to a choice, the more we disregard the social realities surrounding the choice, and the more we refuse to take account of particular attributes of the person making the choice, the more likely we are to judge the actor's choice as free—and vice versa. An extraordinarily telling illustration of the relation between our evaluation of a person's choice or consent and the amount of information we have about the setting in which that "choice" was made comes from O'Brien v. Cunard S.S. Co.,[9] a century-old decision that appears in several tort casebooks in the chapter on the defense of consent to a claim for battery.

Mary O'Brien sued Cunard Steam-Ship Company for personal injury resulting from a smallpox vaccination she received from the ship's surgeon while emigrating from Ireland to the United States. One of Ms. O'Brien's claims against the surgeon and company was for battery, an intentional, unprivileged infliction of harmful or offensive contact. The defendants raised the defense of consent, which, if proven, would defeat her claim. Consent is legally established if Ms. O'Brien manifested consent, that is, if a reasonable person in the shoes of the surgeon would have believed that Ms. O'Brien was actually willing to be vaccinated. Both the trial and appellate courts in O'Brien weighed the circumstances of Ms. O'Brien's vaccination and ruled that it was so obvious that she had manifested consent that reasonable minds could not differ. Thus, the courts did not permit Ms. O'Brien to get her case to a jury of her peers (more than a few of which almost surely would have been Irish); instead, they ruled that she consented to the vaccination as a matter of law.

When my students first read the court's opinion in *O'Brien*, most wholeheartedly endorse the court's conclusions. Given the way the Supreme Judicial Court of Massachusetts frames Ms. O'Brien's story, it is easy to see why. According to the court, on the day Ms. O'Brien was vaccinated, "about two hundred women passengers were assembled below" deck. The surgeon lined them up, examined each for a mark, inoculated all those who had no marks, provided each with a card, and let them go back on deck. Signs were posted around the ship stating that only vaccinated persons could freely land, and that anyone aboard ship who failed to prove that they had been vaccinated (proof of vaccination could consist of a mark from a previous vaccination) must be vaccinated by the ship's surgeon or else face a fourteen-day quarantine on shore. In the court's view, no one "assembled below" objected, and everyone's conduct evinced a desire to take advantage of the surgeon's services. I quote the most crucial part of the court's version of the transaction:

> By [her] testimony, . . . it appears that . . . when her turn
> came she showed him her arm; he looked at it, and said there
> was no mark, and that she should be vaccinated; that she told
> him she had been vaccinated before, and it left no mark; "that
> he then said nothing; that he should vaccinate her again;"
> that she held up her arm to be vaccinated; that no one touched
> her; that she did not tell him she did not want to be vacci-
> nated; and that she took the ticket which he gave . . . and used
> it at quarantine.

Thus summarizing the record, the court held that all reasonable minds must agree that Ms. O'Brien freely chose to be vaccinated, that is, she consented.

For my students, the most compelling part of the court's

story is where Ms. O'Brien "held up her arm to be vaccinated" when the surgeon, without touching her, said that he "should vaccinate her again." "What more compelling proof of consent to such a procedure can there be," my students query, "than for a person to hold up her arm without ever saying she does not want to be inoculated?" The court's finding of consent seems obvious to the point of banality once we adopt its narrative.

Before informing my students of key aspects of the narrative that the court left out, I correct a basic and commonplace flaw in the students' logic. "Just because one submits to the demands of another does not mean that the person consents to those demands, does it?" I query rhetorically. "If someone points a gun at you and says 'you should give me your wallet,' you would not say that your act of handing over your wallet—your choice to give him the wallet rather than risk a bullet—was a consensual act, a free choice, would you?" The students immediately comprehend that focusing too narrowly on a transaction without considering its setting undermines clear thinking about consent and choice. To be sure, at the instant I hand over my wallet to the assailant, I am "actually willing" to part company with it—I may be choosing the lesser of available evils, but at the moment of transfer I am exercising choice. If we narrowly freeze-frame the transaction at the moment of transfer and crop out the rest of the context, my act looks perfectly intentional, consensual, and freely willed. This interpretation of the transaction dissolves, however, as soon as we broaden the time frame and attend to more of the context.

I then draw on the trial record and attorneys' briefs in O'Brien to supply my students with the details that the court's opinion leaves out. From the trial record we learn that Mary O'Brien was a seventeen-year-old Irish emigrant traveling with her father and younger brother to Boston in steerage, the cheapest possible accommodations on a passenger ship. Ms. O'Brien was poor, unsophisticated, and not very educated (she did not understand the meaning of the terms "quarantine" and "vaccinate" when she read them on the signs posted around the ship).

The steerage steward told the two hundred Irish women steerage passengers who were on deck that they had to go below into steerage, without telling them why. (At another point, the male Irish steerage passengers were told to go down into steerage and were "hosed down before they knew what was to be done.") There was only one way out of the steerage area, a door at the top of a staircase. At the middle of the staircase stood a landing occupied by the doctor and two steerage stewards. There was no other exit. The women were lined up in such a way that they could not leave until they had been examined. One of the steerage stewards stood in front of the door leading to the deck so that no one could leave without the surgeon's order.

Mary O'Brien, separated from her father for the first time, nervously avoided getting in line until all the other women had been examined by the doctor and passed through the door leading to the deck. She was left standing alone—this member of a despised "race"[10]—in a dim narrow passageway, surrounded by three domineering men clothed in authority. She told the doctor that she had been vaccinated before. He retorted that she "must" be vaccinated. (Although the court's opinion states that the doctor said that she "should" be vaccinated, Ms. O'Brien testified that he said she "must" be vaccinated.) In such a situation, is it so overwhelmingly obvious that Ms. O'Brien's submission to the surgeon's command expressed her free will that she should be denied a jury of her peers for their opinion on the matter?

My students find these additional narrative facts sobering and disquieting. Sobering because the additional facts indicate a threatening and coercive situation, marked by a menacing show of force and an absence of options for Ms. O'Brien. Disquieting because the additional facts reveal a picture very different from the one conjured in the court's decontextualized opinion. My students learn early the power of narrative and the capacity of courts to achieve a desired outcome by manipulating the terms of narrative. The notion of law as a body of universal rules that determine the outcomes of disputes dissolves when they see that the framing of legal narrative determines these outcomes at least as much as the underlying substantive rules. Because few rules exist for how judges should frame narratives, this means there is a great deal of indeterminacy and room for bias at the heart of the legal process. *O'Brien* gives many of my students their first taste of the fruit of the tree of realist legal knowledge—a fruit that for some is bitter and disenchanting, but for others is ripe with the promise of deeper insight.

### The Fundamental Fault Line: Determinism versus Antideterminism

Thus, the battle over context and perspective really boils down to one over how we should think about choice. And the battle over alternative conceptions of choice, in turn, is really a clash of antideterminist versus determinist explanations of human behavior. By "antideterminism" I mean the principle that people freely choose their actions and thus are completely responsible for what they do. By "determinism" I mean the principle that human behavior can be understood as the product of prior causal events. For the determinist, we are all enmeshed in a web of sometimes compelling, sometimes subtle, and often unconscious influences that renders talk of any kind of pristine free choice vacuous.

Much resistance to women's self-defense work stems from worry over the subversive implications of openly acknowledging the deep connections among context, perspective, and choice. Acknowledging these connections weakens the purely antideterminist approach to criminal incidents by inviting a more searching investigation of the harsh circumstances that may have conditioned a defendant's "decision" to violate a legal norm. But admitting that criminal acts may be determined (at least partially) by unjust environmental pressures undermines our ability self-righteously to demonize people who commit crimes, challenges the presumed link between blame and punishment, and compels us to reconsider the cruelty of the punishments we mete out. Is it any wonder, then, that mainstream commentators shrink from the proposal of even modest determinist doctrines in the criminal law?

For a revealing example of the unwarranted panic that determinist approaches to human behavior strikes in the heart of traditional criminal scholars, consider their reaction to a modest proposal by Richard Delgado, a prominent legal thinker, that the criminal law should recognize an excuse for persons whose crimes were induced by coercive persuasion, popularly known as brainwashing.[11] Under Delgado's proposal, the defense was to be limited to persons whose mental state had been forcibly altered by brutal external pressures applied by a powerful captor. Moreover, the defense could not be invoked by someone who voluntarily joined the group that allegedly brainwashed him or whose condition could otherwise be attributed to some "choice" on his part.

Despite the limited scope of Delgado's proposal, Joshua Dressler, a noted mainstream legal thinker, warned that recognizing such an excuse threatened the collapse of the entire system of criminal blaming! According to Dressler, recognizing Delgado's excuse would put us on a slippery slope, inevitably leading to recognition of a universal excuse based on the influence of external circumstances on an accused's choice.[12] Dressler ends his apocalyptic critique by chiding Delgado for ignoring the dire implications of his revolutionary suggestion.

My first thought upon reading Dressler's exaggerated rebuke of Delgado's modest proposal took the form of a paraphrase of a line from Shakespeare—the gentleman doth protest too much. In other words, such overreactions to severely limited deterministic proposals bespeak the sway of ideology. Of course, most positions on controversial topics are rooted in some political ideology. But mainstream legal thinkers vehemently deny this truism. They see themselves as objectively balancing competing considerations and reaching meticulously reasoned results.

My second response was a deepened sense of awe at the achievements of advocates for battered women, for these activists had to overcome this kind of shrill and obdurate opposition to determinist perspectives before they could get courts to admit evidence of "battered woman's syndrome."[13] Finally, my third response was to canvass mentally the numerous determinist doctrines the law has recognized for many years without precipitating the collapse of the entire system of criminal blaming. For example, the commentary to Section 2.09 or the Model Penal Code explains the operation of duress doctrine with the following illustration:

(a) X is unwillingly driving a car along a narrow and precipitous mountain road, falling off sharply on both sides, under
the command of Y, an armed escaping felon. The headlights
pick out two persons, apparently and actually drunk, lying
across the road in such a position as to make passage impossible without running them over. X is prevented from stopping by the threat of Y to shoot him dead if he declines to
drive straight on. If X does go on and kills the drunks in order
to save himself he will be excused [under duress doctrine] if
the jury should find that "a person of reasonable firmness in
his situation would have been unable to resist," although he
would not be justified under the lesser evil principle of
[necessity doctrine].

X's choice in this hypothetical situation to kill the people
lying across the road rather than sacrifice himself is deemed to
be determined. Whenever a court recognizes a defense of duress,
it is acknowledging that a person cannot be condemned for
choosing to break the law until more is known about the roots
of his or her choice. And to assess the roots of that choice, the
time frame must be broadened beyond the moment of the criminal incident itself and the choice evaluated in view of the situation in which the criminal incident occurred.

Provocation is another determinist doctrine that courts routinely recognize. For instance, a husband or wife (in practice,
provocation excuses have been most successfully invoked by husbands) who discovers a spouse in the act of committing adultery
and kills the spouse or paramour may seek to reduce his or her
criminal liability from murder to voluntary manslaughter. At the
moment of the killing, the defendant intends[14] to kill the spouse,
but courts hold that "in spite of the existence of this bad intent the
circumstances may reduce the homicide to manslaughter."[15]

Again, provocation doctrine directs fact finders to look behind the decision to kill to its causes,[16] and to ask whether the circumstances leading up to it would excite the passion of a reasonable person. If they answer yes, then the killing is partially excused.

What drives these and other determinist doctrines is the insight that in certain cases decision makers cannot make the usual inference that a person is blameworthy from the fact that he chose to break the law.[17] These excuses turn on the recognition that the defendant's extraordinary circumstances drove a wedge between his contingent self—the self that came forward under the unjust pressures of the situation in which he found himself—and some underlying "true" self that could have manifested itself but for those unjust pressures.[18] As Martin Wasik puts it, in cases of duress "the accused claims that there was no act by *him*."[19] By this logic, it is unfair unconditionally to condemn someone for the behavior of his contingent self, for the responses of this unduly influenced self do not tell us anything about the defendant's "true" character. And we must ascertain an individual's true character before we can hold him fully responsible for criminal acts.

This rationale neatly explains the determinist doctrines that the courts recognize; but what courts and commentators do not adequately explain is why these doctrines are so strictly limited. Generally, courts strictly cabin the duress defense by requiring that the defendant face immediate and specific threats, usually of death or severe bodily injury,[20] and that the threats come from specific human agents who seek to compel the defendant to commit the particular crime for which he is charged.[21] The Model Penal Code illustrates the strictness of these restrictions on the duress defense in the following variation on their earlier hypothetical situation:

(b) The same situation as above except that X is prevented from stopping by suddenly inoperative brakes. His alternatives are either to run down the drunks or to run off the road and down the mountainside. If X chooses the first alternative to save his own life and kills the drunks he will not be excused under [duress doctrine] even if a jury should find that a person of reasonable fortitude would have been unable to do otherwise.[22]

From the standpoint of the defendant's blameworthiness (the sine qua non of just punishment for the retributionist), it is impossible to distinguish between these two hypothetical situations. In both cases the defendant faces equally severe and immediate external pressures compelling him to commit the same crime. His decision to run over the people lying across the road tells us no more about his "true" character in the second situation than in the first. And the following distinction between the two cases offered in the commentary to the Model Penal Code is embarrassingly strained: "In the former situation, the basic interests of the law may be satisfied by prosecution of the agent of unlawful force; in the latter circumstance, if the actor is excused, no one is subject to the law's application."[23]

### "Disadvantaged Social Background"

Why does the excuse of duress cause mainstream thinkers to grasp at such threadbare distinctions to keep it rigidly restricted? The reason—openly confessed by mainstream academics[24]—is because determinist doctrines like duress severely threaten the coherence and cogency of the intentionalist assumptions of ordinary criminal law discourse. Once we admit that decisions to break the law are sometimes blameless because those decisions are determined by preceding factors, and once we acknowledge that in some cases we must inquire into the roots of bad intentions and choices to evaluate blameworthiness, we naturally begin to wonder why we do not inquire into the roots of decisions to break the law in *all* criminal cases. Why not always broaden the time frame and consider the impact of background circumstances on a defendant's capacity to choose? For example, why not weigh the impact of a disadvantaged social background on a defendant's criminal behavior in all cases in which the defendant comes from such a background?

Judge David Bazelon proposed just such a defense, first in a separate court opinion in 1972[25] and then in a law review article a few years later.[26] Bazelon's proposal grew out of his assessment that a number of defendants suffered the same kinds of cognitive and volitional defects that constitute excuses in cases where mental illness is found, but that they could not meet some of the technical requirements of the definition of legal insanity. Upon further reflection, Judge Bazelon realized that the mental impairments afflicting these defendants were the product of social, economic, and cultural deprivations or of racial discrimination, rather than of a clinically defined mental illness. Accordingly, he proposed a jury instruction that would permit acquittal where the crime was caused by the defendant's disadvantaged background. Specifically, he would instruct the jury to acquit if it found that, at the time of the offense, the defendant's "mental or emotional processes or behavior controls were impaired to such an extent that he cannot justly be held responsible for his act."[27] Although Judge Bazelon did not expect that his new instruction would generate a flood of new acquittals,[28] he hoped the instruction would force jurors to confront the causes of criminal behavior and thus compel the community to own up to its responsibility for the crime and for the plight of the accused. In Judge Bazelon's words, "It is simply unjust to place people in dehumanizing social conditions, to do nothing about those conditions, and then to command those who suffer, 'Behave—or else!'"

Given the near-hysterical reaction to Richard Delgado's carefully circumscribed brainwashing excuse, it is not hard to imagine the thundering chorus of scholarly condemnation— still reverberating today—that greeted Judge Bazelon's disadvantaged social background excuse. The question, however, that none of Judge Bazelon's critics coherently answer is *why* courts can recognize the restricted determinism of duress or provocation but not the fuller determinism of the disadvantaged social background excuse. As far as what a person's choice does or does not reveal about that person's "true" character, what difference does it make whether his choice to do wrong is rooted in an immediate threat from an armed assailant (restricted determinism) or a brutally abusive childhood (fuller determinism)? In pondering this question, we must fully contemplate the desperate plight of battered children: "Victims of child abuse are likely to be kids from poor and often profoundly twisted families. They live in nightmare worlds of filth and hunger and violence and extreme pain. Often their [lives] are case studies in unrelieved torment, sickening to hear about, sordid beyond belief."[29]

### Opponents Grasp at Straws

George Fletcher, author of *With Justice for Some: Victims' Rights in Criminal Trials*, is a leading champion of popular demands for conviction and tougher punishment under the misleading label of "victims' rights." Because he offers as sophisticated an account as can be found of why the law should not recognize a disadvantaged social background excuse, we shall focus on his arguments as representative of the antideterminist, just-deserts school of blame and punishment.[30] He makes several different arguments against a social deprivation excuse. He begins his first argument with the now familiar point that legitimate excuses arise from atypical circumstances that make it impossible for us to infer anything about the defendant's "true character" from his wrongful act.[31] Then he says that whether a particular wrongful act is attributable to a defendant's character or to the circumstances that impaired his capacity for choice is a question that can be answered in an either/or way. He concludes that the problem with excuses based on social deprivation is that these excuses "interweave" these two distinct ways of accounting for wrongful behavior.

Merely asserting that wrongful acts can always be attributed either to a person's "true character" or to his circumstances does nothing to advance the claim that we should ignore background conditions of deprivation in determining whether a wrongful act reveals someone's "true character." Could any of us presume to know the "true character" of a child who suffers unremitting rape or torture throughout his childhood? Then how can any of us presume to know that the wrongful acts of a former battered child reveal his "true character?"

It is no answer to say that because not every former battered child commits similar wrongful acts, the wrongful acts of this particular battered child reveal his truly blameworthy character. For not every spouse who discovers adultery in progress kills the adulterous mate. (In fact, the law presumes that the ordinary person would never be provoked to take another life under any circumstances, which is why provocation is not a complete defense.)[32] Nevertheless, we view the decision to kill under such circumstances as significantly determined and thus partially excused because we think such circumstances make the ordinary person *more likely* to kill.[33] Hence, a defendant who appeals to excusing conditions in his defense does not have to prove that most people who were exposed to those same conditions would have committed a similar act. All he or she has to show is that because of those excusing conditions, the wrongful act does not reveal his "true character."

Fletcher also tries to distinguish the restricted determinism reflected in traditional duress doctrine from the fuller determinism of a disadvantaged social background by asserting that someone like our former battered child was still free to choose the particulars of the crime he ultimately committed.[34] According to this argument, traditional sources of duress, such as the bank robbers in our earlier hypotheticals, induce a person to commit a particular crime, such as turning over the bank's money to a stranger or running over unconscious people in the road. But a person's "nightmare world of filth and hunger and violence and extreme pain" does not induce him to perpetrate the particular crimes he ultimately engages in. Thus, the wrongful act of the former battered child—because its particulars are chosen "freely"—is more blameworthy than the wrongful act of the victims of the bank robbers.

The freedom to choose the particulars of a wrongful act does not necessarily make the actor more blameworthy, however. If the bank robber orders the teller to steal a getaway car on pain of dire consequences for the teller's infant daughter, the teller is not more blameworthy for succumbing to the robber's demands merely because he can "freely" choose the kind of car to steal and from whom to steal it. Nor is the driver more blameworthy for driving over two unconscious persons if the robber with the gun to his head lets him choose which of three precipitous mountain roads to take, all of which contain unconscious bodies lying across them. Similarly, a person under extraordinary pressures to commit crimes is not necessarily more blameworthy because he or she has some choice as to which crimes to commit and in what manner.

Perhaps recognizing the irremediable slipperiness of the distinctions between character and circumstances, and between choosing and not choosing the particulars of a crime, Fletcher resorts to popular assumptions, hoary conventions, and unabashed complacency for support. Because his argument here epitomizes the smugly conservative rhetoric that marks mainstream reactions to the disadvantaged social background excuse, I quote it in full:

> The arguments against excusing too many wrongdoers are both moral and institutional. The moral or philosophical argument is addressed to the problem of determinism and responsibility in the standard cases of wrongdoing. *It is difficult to resolve this issue except by noting that we all blame and criticize others, and in turn subject ourselves to blame and criticism, on the assumption of responsibility for our conduct.* In order to defend the criminal law against the determinist critique, we need not introduce freighted terms like "freedom of the will." Nor need we "posit" freedom as though we were developing a geometric system on the basis of axioms. *The point is simply that the criminal law should express the way we live. Our culture is built on the assumption that, absent valid claims of excuse, we are accountable for what we do.* If that cul-

tural presupposition should someday prove to be empirically false, there will be far more radical changes in our way of life than those expressed in the criminal law.[35]

This argument contains numerous deep flaws. First, its primary jurisprudential premise that the criminal law—or any other branch of the law, for that matter—should merely reflect popular assumptions and "express the way we live" is wrong. This was the position of the Reasonable Racist! Popular assumptions sometimes reflect nothing more than ingrained stereotypes, and the way we *actually* live may contradict our aspirations for the way we *ought* to live. To vindicate important values such as racial and sexual equality, courts frequently make decisions that challenge prevailing stereotypes and disrupt "the way we live." If popular assumptions about personal responsibility contradict important moral norms (such as it is unfair to punish someone for a wrongful act unless it reveals his "true character"), it is within the province of the courts to focus the community's attention on the contradiction by recognizing an excuse that forces jurors, sitting as representatives of the community, to confront this contradiction in reaching their verdict.

Furthermore, the assertion that "[o]ur culture is built on the assumption that, absent valid claims of excuse, we are accountable for what we do" is tautological. The argument merely states that "our culture holds actors accountable unless they are excused." But such a statement begs the fundamental question: What constitutes a valid claim of excuse, and does social deprivation qualify? If "our culture" is also built on the moral norm that only the blameworthy are justly punished (as Fletcher elsewhere says that it is),[36] then social deprivation might qualify as one of "our cultures" "valid claims of excuse."

Finally, the argument that "[i]t is difficult to resolve [the problem of determinism and responsibility] except by noting that we all blame and criticize others, and in turn subject ourselves to blame and criticism, on the assumption of responsibility for our conduct," merely asserts that "'our culture' (*whose* culture?) holds certain people accountable because that's what we have always done."[37] When all else fails, appeal to complacency as cavalierly as possible and disdain further discussion. Disadvantaged and socially marginalized groups have especially good reason to regard such arguments with suspicion, for "what we have always done" has produced and continues to perpetuate their desperate plight.

### Ideological Agendas

In the end, one must wonder what it is about deterministic perspectives that compels otherwise able writers like Fletcher to lapse into empty tautologies and proudly complacent assertions in seeking to refute them. This zealous advocacy of antideterminist perspectives along with the inconsistent but vociferous denunciations of determinist ones serves and reflects a host of ideological agendas.

First, it is easier to rationalize the cruelty of our current practices if we self-righteously condemn the men and women we either lock up or kill. To self-righteously condemn, however, we must first convince ourselves that we can divine the "true character" of the accused. If we humbly admit that we lack the omniscience to divine a person's "true character," especially when that person has lived though oppressive or brutally dehumanizing circumstances, we could give a more human face to criminals ("there but for the grace of god go I") rather than demonizing

them. Although we could still incarcerate individuals who harm
others for the sake of deterrence or rehabilitation, we could no
longer applaud hanging, shooting, electrocuting, or lethally
injecting other human beings in the name of justice.

Notwithstanding the lust for revenge that largely drives the
"victims' rights" bandwagon on which many politicians and
academics have recently jumped, a growing number of former
victims of serious crimes are publicly advocating compassion,
humility, and healing. Anne Coleman, for example, held a vigil
in the cold outside the Delaware Correctional Facility on January 25, 1996 when a double-murderer, Billy Bailey, died at the
end of a rope. She was joined by one hundred other opponents
of the death penalty. Mrs. Coleman prayed and protested for Mr.
Bailey even though she lost her own daughter at the hands of an
anonymous murderer eleven years earlier. She could never for-
get the stench of her own daughter's blood in the car where she
was shot, or the sight of her body in the county morgue. Nevertheless, she cannot condone killing in the name of justice. "I've
always been horrified by violence," Mrs. Coleman said in an
interview hours before the hanging. "No matter if it is a
stranger or the state doing the killing, it is wrong."[38]

Mrs. Coleman is one of three thousand members of a nation-
wide group, Murder Victims' Families for Reconciliation, that
actively opposes the death penalty even though most members
have had a loved one murdered. Group members have buried
their children but not their capacity for compassion and mercy.
Their personal experiences with murder and grief foreclose
attempts to label them as "bleeding hearts." For the last few
years the group has conducted speaking tours, sharing their
message of forgiveness with a country clamoring for bloody
vengeance. A few days after the state hanged Billy Bailey, Mrs.

Coleman and fellow members of Murder Victims Family were standing outside of the prison in the cold again, praying and protesting the imminent execution of yet another inmate. "We'll be back again and again," Mrs. Coleman said, "until we break this cycle of violence and replace it with healing."[39]

Astonishingly, although Mrs. Coleman and other members of Murder Victims Family seem heroic in their capacity for compassion, some defenders of popular punitive approaches to blame and punishment contend that our feelings of sympathy for the disadvantaged persons whom Judge Bazelon would excuse actually grow out of a sense of "elitism" and "condescension" rather than altruism. One leading mainstream critic argues that our sympathy for the disadvantaged defendant "betokens a refusal to acknowledge the equal moral dignity of others." In not condemning the "unhappy deviant" from a disadvantaged background, he asserts, we imply that he is not expected to live up to the same "high moral standards" by which we judge ourselves and that he is a less complete human being than ourselves.[40] Similarly, another prominent critic attacks Judge Bazelon's proposal on the ground that such an excuse treats the accused person as "an infant, a machine, or an animal."[41] "Those who propose this defense," he continues, "are plainly moved by compassion for the downtrodden, to whom, however, it is nonetheless an insult."[42]

The problem with this critique of the social deprivation excuse is that it proves too much. For the logic of this critique applies just as well to the defenses of duress and provocation—determinist doctrines that mainstream commentators fully endorse. Thus, why not attribute our feelings of sympathy for the "unhappy deviant" who, in the heat of passion, kills his spouse—or who runs over three unconscious individuals to save his own neck—to a sense of "elitism" or "condescension" that implies "the unhappy deviant" is not expected to live up to the same "high moral standards" by which we judge ourselves?

One circular and self-serving response to this question would be: "We do expect the person who violates the law under duress or provocation to live up to the same 'high moral standards' by which we judge ourselves. It's just that the 'high moral standards' by which we currently judge ourselves—and according to which we carve out our currently recognized legal excuses—make allowances only for short-run pressures that immediately precede the crime for which the defendant stands accused. Long-term background pressures of the kind generated by a bleak and oppressive social background simply do not count in our 'high moral standards' and corresponding legal excuses." The problem with this response is that the "official" expositors of "our" "high moral standards," and especially those officials who determine which excuses are legally valid, are neither impartial nor objective. They do not stand behind a Rawlsian veil of ignorance that masks information about the their own background when deciding which excuses to recognize. They already know that they do not have to worry about the emotional and psychological effects of a desperately impoverished and brutal social background, because the vast majority of them already have reached adulthood without having to face "nightmare worlds of filth and hunger and violence and extreme pain." In contrast, they are as likely as anyone to surprise a cheating spouse *in flagrante delicto* or encounter the various other short-run immediate pressures of the kind that constitute duress and provocation. Thus, it is in their interest to defend the excuses that may benefit them while dismissing excuses that require pressures that are beyond their reach.

Anytime a body of rules drawn to protect certain interests but not others (as all rules inevitably are) is administered by people who already know what their interests are and where they lie, it can come as no surprise to find rampant definitional gerrymandering in favor of the administrators' own interests. Mark Kelman, an important critical legal thinker, nicely illustrates the dynamics of such gerrymandering with the following loose analogy:

> A large social group is setting up a massive health insurance, risk-pooling plan. Should treating hemophilia be included? Since hemophilia is a purely hereditary ailment, everyone will know whether he faces high bills for the disease. Purely selfish insurance purchasers will exclude the disease from coverage. If the defense of duress is "insurance" against being blamed or incarcerated, the dominant social group will exclude "long-term pressures" as a covered syndrome since they already know they will not be afflicted.[43]

What is so disturbing about this gerrymandering dynamic at the heart of the law is not so much that it happens at all (because line drawing lies at the heart of any body of rules, any legal system is liable to definitional gerrymandering), but that it is so insistently denied. If mainstream commentators admitted that our blaming and excusing practices turn not on objective moral truth, but rather on political, ideological, and even social psychological grounds, we could honestly reevaluate the fairness of our current approaches to crime and punishment. Central to this reevaluation would be recognition of our tendency systematically to ignore or undervalue the interests of socially marginalized groups in framing laws and meting out punishment. I have confidence, born of empirical research, that once we admit our discriminatory tendencies, we can combat them. But we cannot combat what we deny or ignore.

It is striking and revealing to note the parallels between the rhetoric employed by the mainstream critics who attacked Bazelon's social deprivation excuse and the rhetoric employed by many critics of affirmative action. Recall the first critic's admonition that in not condemning the "unhappy deviant" from a disadvantaged background, we imply that he is not expected to live up to the same high standards by which we judge ourselves. And recall the other critic's contention that those who propose that we make allowances for a person's disadvantaged social background "are plainly moved by compassion for the downtrodden, to whom, however, it is nonetheless an insult." This same rhetoric is often employed by opponents of affirmative action who argue that public policy intervention to rectify Black mobility difficulties deviates from the pure-merit or just-deserts approach to allocating opportunities and thereby demeans its beneficiaries.

These rhetorical similarities are more than coincidental. They reflect a common ideological anxiety by the dominant group about the coherence of "just deserts" justifications for the prevailing social distribution of rewards as well as punishments. For once we admit that our ordinary conventions for attributing blame to others are biased and logically incoherent, we start to suffer nagging doubts about whether the ones we use for attributing merit are just as biased and self-serving. Put differently, one implication of a decision to excuse wrongdoing on the ground that our misconduct may be determined (at least partially) by environmental factors is that our achievements also may be attributed (again, at least partially) to those same factors rather than simply to personal choice and hard work. This relation between popular conceptions of blame and self-congratulatory conceptions of merit is aptly described in the following passage by Nathan Caplan and Stephen Nelson:

> Person-blame interpretations reinforce social myths about one's degree of control over his own fate, thus rewarding the members of the great middle class by flattering their self-esteem for having "made it on their own." This in turn increases public complacency about the plight of those who have not "made it on their own."[44]

The affirmative action debate also provides another illustration of the dominant group's tendency to condone practices that promote its own interests while hypocritically condemning analogous practices that primarily promote the interests of marginalized groups. For example, arrangements that go beyond considerations of "pure merit" in job recruitment and job entry are endemic to the American job market. (To flesh out this point, I will assume the extremely dubious proposition that currently accepted tests and credentials actually measure "merit.") These arrangements include "a buddy network among, say, lawyers, managers, academics; assistance from upper-class status networks or cliques; the assistance of an ethnic-bloc congressional network; and even government policies [including tax cuts and subsidies] favoring targeted groups like veterans, businesses, or agricultural producers."[45] Rarely are these pervasive forms of preferential assistance criticized as assaults on the pure-merit paradigm. Occasionally one hears grumblings about "corporate welfare," but such subsidies are only the tip of the iceberg—the other forms of preferential assistance that disproportionately benefit White males constitute the vast but unacknowledged antarctic of White affirmative action.[46]

In stark contrast, affirmative action programs that help women, Blacks, and Hispanics gain access to certain job markets and educational institutions from which they were undemocratically excluded are singled out for condemnation as cases of "reverse discrimination." Moreover, Black conservatives insist that the Black beneficiaries of affirmative action should feel self-doubt and moral ambiguity, yet innumerable White male businessmen, farmers, builders, bankers, and arms manufacturers have gained affirmative assistance benefits without expressing the slightest self-doubt about having gained such benefits. In the end, the hypocritical denouncement of affirmative action for socially marginalized groups reflects political interests, not objective moral judgments.

The debate over affirmative action in college admissions is also shrouded in hypocrisy. Affirmative action for women and minorities in college admissions is routinely characterized by critics as "reverse discrimination." Yet one rarely if ever hears these same critics level their righteous indignation about violations of the pure-merit paradigm at the other large group of beneficiaries of special consideration in college admissions—namely, "legacies." "Legacies" are the children of alumni, and they enjoy a huge edge in the admissions process. According to the *Wall Street Journal*, "The percentage [of legacies] accepted at most selective colleges is often more than twice that of the general pool of candidates."[47] To convey an idea of how admissions decisions are made at selective schools, one selective college agreed to let a staff reporter for the *Journal* sit in on deliberations. The reporter's description of the operation of this predominately and *disproportionately White* form of affirmative action is telling:

At Amherst, each [legacy] receives a "pink sheet" rating for the parents' support of the college in work such as admissions interviewing and fund-raising, and also for financial contributions. Problems occur when the pink sheet is "hot" and the candidate isn't.

In late February, as the staffers winnow the stack of applications prior to committee work, they are already struggling. "She's a dull kid. She wasn't so bad in interview, but these essays . . . ," Mr. Thibourot says of one applicant. "The only reason she's staying in is she's a.d.," he adds, using office shorthand for "alumni daughter."

In committee, rejecting an applicant with "hot pink" is more difficult. "We've got one that'll have to go up the hill," Mr. Bedford says, meaning that the staff will talk to the college president before making a decision likely to draw angry protests. "You can't let the head office get blindsided," Mr. Bedford explains.[48]

The irony here is that foes of affirmative action for historically marginalized groups vigorously contend that the marginalized status of one's ancestors should not matter in the present-day allocation of opportunities. Yet in the well-established and prevalent practice of legacy admissions, decision makers directly review the privileged status of the applicant's ancestors (who must have been enrolled in host institution) for purposes of allocating scarce opportunities. To be sure, these decision makers also consider the ancestors' current efforts to help the host institution, but these considerations only come into play after the ancestors have satisfied the threshold status requirement of having graduated from the school. With legacies, the selfishly selective condemnation process seems to boil down to this: If allocating benefits on the basis of the status of a person's ancestors primarily benefits the dominant group, the principle of allocation escapes serious criticism; but if the primary beneficiaries are from subordinate groups, the principle of allocation comes under withering attack as "reverse discrimination."

I must note a twist in the story of the University of California regents' assault on affirmative action that underscores the first-degree hypocrisy practiced by many antiaffirmative action activists. After many regents sanctimoniously denounced affirmative action in higher education and voted it out of existence in the California system, a *Los Angeles Times* investigation revealed that several regents—as well as state politicians vocally opposed to affirmative action—used their influence to get relatives, friends, and the children of their business associates into UCLA. (See, e.g., "UCLA Chief Admits Possible Favoritism; Chancellor Charles Young Acknowledges Applicants Sponsored by Regents and Other Officials May Have Been Given Admissions Preferences," *Los Angeles Times*, March 17, 1996, at page 3.)

Another reason many shrink at determinist perspectives is that such perspectives shift the focus in a case from the individual actor to the harsh circumstances in which she found herself and to the fact that her crime may be (at least partly) attributable to those circumstances. Many start to squirm when responsibility for a problem is traced to social, economic, and political circumstances, because this implies that responsibility may ultimately rest with those of us who help maintain those circumstances. Many of us would rather scapegoat the victims of untoward circumstances than share any responsibility for their victimization and its consequences. An instructive example of this scapegoating tendency comes from a borrowed exercise I go through with my students.

Consider the following thought experiment created by Judge Guido Calabresi.[49] Imagine you are the most powerful decision maker in a large community and that I am an Evil Deity. As the Evil Deity, I propose to you a Faustian exchange: You can choose anything you want (I care not how hedonistic or idealistic, so long as it does not save lives), and in return I get to randomly execute one thousand of your most robust citizens in gruesome ways. Do you accept my offer? When I offer this deal to my students, I generally get no takers and a measure of indignation that I could even make such an indecent proposal. Then I ask them to distinguish between the boon I just hypothetically offered and the automobile, which every year takes over forty thousand lives, usually in gruesome, excruciating ways.

Students strive mightily to come up with distinctions, none of which really hold up under scrutiny, but one of which is directly relevant to choice and scapegoating. "In the hypothetical situation," they argue, "the powerful decision maker is responsible for the deaths rather than the victims because the decision maker alone cuts the deal with the devil and chooses the boon for everyone. But with cars the victims choose the boon for themselves; the decision to get behind the wheel is a voluntary one. When people freely choose to run certain risks, they have to live with the consequences of their choices. If they are killed or injured, they have assumed those risks."

Assuming free choice entails full responsibility, the problem is that choice can be so limited by circumstances as to be more illusory than real. We as a society cannot escape responsibility for maintaining circumstances that allow for only illusory choice. For example, social and economic existence in this society is now predominately organized around motor vehicles. Shopping, employment opportunities, and other core community activities are located in places that most people cannot reach without using some kind of motor vehicle. How real is a choice between gainful employment on the one hand, and not using motorized transportation on the other? Theoretically, a person could forswear all contemporary social and economic institutions, bid adieu to friends and family, and revert to a preindustrial existence herding sheep. However, we must stretch the meaning of "meaningful choice" beyond recognition to say that such options are consistent with free choice.

Moreover, we as a society are responsible for the limited range of options available to people who do not want to accept the boon of motor vehicles. Through our elected representatives (including zoning boards) and consumer behavior, we make collective decisions about the construction and expansion of highways, the location of business districts, and the placement of shopping malls. How fair is it to create collectively a situation in which an individual's choice is so limited as to border on illusory and then point to that illusory "choice" as grounds for imposing full responsibility on the individual? To do so is to indulge in scapegoating.

Ugly scapegoating also infects popular perceptions of battered women. Hearing that a woman repeatedly "chose" to return to or stay in a battering relationship, some (perhaps many) conclude that she masochistically invited further beatings, or at least "assumed the risk" of them. In either case, she— and not her circumstances—is held fully responsible for her "choice" not to leave. And she alone is held responsible for the fatal consequences of her "choice." To consider the possibility that her choice was severely constrained or illusory requires us to factor her circumstances into our assignment of responsibility, which may ultimately mean accepting some responsibility *ourselves* for what happened to her and the person she killed. For example, assume that (as often happens in these cases) the battered woman kept going back because of economic dependency, or out of fear for her safety and the safety of her children: Who is responsible for the discrimination against women in the workplace that breeds such economic dependency? Who is responsible for the failure of courts and police to protect battered women who want to leave—a failure that results in thousands of stalkings and deadly separation assaults each year? Perhaps we as a society bear responsibility. But owning up to our collective responsibility for the plight of battered women deprives us of the moral purchase self-righteously to condemn them for their so-called choices.

Our collective flight from responsibility also explains our punitive attitude toward lawbreakers from Black and Latino communities. We as a society are currently running pell-mell from our collective responsibility for the plight of the oppressed and the crime that oppression demonstrably breeds. Numerous studies link crime rates to poverty and unemployment. Corroborating this link—and destroying any genetic explanations of the disproportionate involvement of minorities in crime—is that Blacks who move into the middle class in this country have crime and delinquency rates indistinguishable from those of Whites of the same socioeconomic circumstances.[50] In a racially discriminatory and increasingly zero-sum economy, the privileges many of us enjoy are purchased at the price of the social and economic oppression of others. Further, people saddled with such oppression, those left behind in our bleak and cynically deindustrialized inner-city neighborhoods, "have crime rates and suffer victimization rates grossly higher than the rest of us."[51] Admitting these truths to ourselves would require us to

accept some responsibility for the orgy of violence that domi-
nates the nightly news. But like a confederation of deadbeat
dads, we want to revel licentiously in the spoils of a casino economy that robs the working poor and deepens the plight of
socially marginalized people, and then disown the inevitable
consequences of our excesses when they come home to roost.

# Chapter Six

# REPEALING THE BLACK TAX: BREAKING THE DISCRIMINATION HABIT

The ideal of a color-blind society has long been promoted as a panacea for the blight of both institutional and private racism. For the sake of neutrality and objectivity, we are told, we must do everything in our power to ignore—or better still, to avoid even noticing—each other's race. Consciously thinking about racial identity in decision making is perceived as likely to lead to either discrimination against the stereotyped group or reverse discrimination in its favor. Attorneys who represent minorities, in particular, have been denounced for urging jurors to reexamine their stereotypical reactions to their clients. Detractors accuse these attorneys of "playing the race card" or "playing to the prejudices of the jury."

A dramatic cinematic depiction of this type of the color-blind perspective, or color-blind formalism, appears in several courtroom scenes in the movie *Philadelphia*. The film—inspired by a true story[1]—concerns a successful gay attorney, Andrew Beckett, who is wrongfully discharged by his law firm because of his sexual orientation. In the following scene, Beckett's attorney is cross-examining a firm employee who was involved in the conspiracy to discharge Beckett wrongfully:

PLAINT. ATTY: Are you a homosexual?

WITNESS: What?

PLAINT. ATTY: Are you a homosexual? Answer the question. Are you a homo? Are you a faggot? . . . fairy . . . booty snatcher . . . rump-roaster. Are you gay?

DEF. ATTY: Where did this come from? [The witness's] sexual orientation has nothing to do with this case.

PLAINT. ATTY: Your honor, everybody in this courtroom is thinking about sexual orientation, you know, sexual preference, whatever you want to call it. Who does what to whom, and how they do it. I mean, they're looking at Andrew Beckett [plaint.], they're thinking about it. They're looking at Mr. Wheeler [senior partner], Ms. Cornini [defense counsel], even you, your honor. They're wondering about it. I mean, hey, trust me, I know that they are looking at me and thinking about it. So let's just get it out in the open, let's, let's get it out of the closet, because this case is not just about AIDS, is it? So let's talk about what this case is really all about, the general public's hatred, our loathing, our fear of homosexuals, and how that climate of hatred and fear translated into the firing of this particular homosexual, my client Andrew Beckett.

JUDGE: In this courtroom, justice is blind to matters of race, creed, color, religion, and sexual orientation.

PLAINT. ATTY: With all due respect your honor, we don't live in
   this courtroom though, do we?

JUDGE: No, we don't. However, as regards this witness, I'm
   going to sustain the defense's objection.

Unfortunately, the "color-blind" formalism exemplified by
this fictional judge's reaction to references to sexual orientation
reflects real-life judicial resistance to attorneys' attempts to bring
the issue of prejudice into the open at trial. ("Color-blind" shall be
used throughout this chapter as a shorthand expression for
efforts to ignore or pretend not to notice that another person
belongs to a stereotyped group, regardless whether the basis of
the stereotype is race, gender, sexual orientation, or the like.) For
example, in *Jackson v. Chicago Transit Authority*,[2] a Black plaintiff brought a negligence action against a municipal corporation
for personal injuries sustained when the bus he boarded collided
with a truck. During his closing argument, the plaintiff's counsel
"alluded to the fact that his client was Negro, as contrasted to the
jurors, the attorneys and the court itself, who were all Cau-
casians." The jury returned a verdict for the plaintiff, but the
appellate court granted the defendants a new trial on the ground
that such a racial reference "should not be made before any tri-
bunal. *It is an unmitigated appeal to prejudice and its effect could
only be destructive of the proper administration of justice.*"[3]

In characterizing the reference by the plaintiff's counsel to his
client's racial identity as a case of playing to the prejudices of the
jury, the *Jackson* court ignores a critical distinction between racial
references that subvert the rationality of the fact-finding process
and racial references that actually enhance the rationality and
fairness of the fact-finding process. Worse still, this court's superficial analysis has gained legitimacy and wide currency through

being endorsed by a number of legal writers.[4] Despite these writers and the *Jackson* decision, however, attorneys frequently challenge fact finders explicitly to resist succumbing to bias in making judgments about members of stereotyped groups. For example, in the recent World Trade Center bombing case, defense attorney Austin Campriello asked the jury to avoid associating stereotypes of Arab and Muslim violence and terrorism with his client.[5] And in a recent capital murder trial, defense attorney Paul Nugent urged the jury not to allow homophobia to distort their deliberations about his client's guilt or innocence.[6]

Thus we have two radically conflicting strategies for helping decision makers achieve greater objectivity: color-blindness versus color-consciousness. Do arguments based on race, sexual preference, or any other characteristic widely used to stereotype individuals necessarily "appeal to prejudice," or instead can some such arguments actually promote the rationality and fairness of the fact-finding process? Does race-consciousness help decision makers avoid imposing the Black tax on African Americans, or does it hike up the tax? Are proactive measures for reducing private discrimination feasible, or must we resign ourselves to the inevitability of biased social judgments? We shall begin our discussion with this last question, for a number of thoughtful and progressive thinkers and activists maintain that prejudice is inevitable. If this rather fatalistic view is correct, we truly shall remain lost in a wilderness of racial injustice, and the dream of Martin Luther King, Jr., shall remain forever deferred.

### Hypocritical Racists and Aversive Racists

Americans share a cultural belief system saturated with derogatory stereotypes about Blacks; thus we have all been influenced by these stereotypes. Does this mean that we are all racists? Leading thinkers in law, psychology, and social science answer this question with an emphatic "yes." They view prejudice as an inevitable outgrowth of our stereotype-ridden cultural belief system.[7]

This view of prejudice as inevitable and ubiquitous, however, does not square with polls and studies indicating that prejudice has been declining steadily over the past forty years. Between 1956 and 1978, reports on attitudes of White Americans toward Black Americans show a steady increase in the percentage of Whites who favor equality for Blacks in all areas of American society.[8] The most common objection to these studies is that they do not capture the resurgence of racism in the late 1980s. A review of studies and surveys conducted between 1984 and 1990 on young White adults, however, showed that there was no significant decline in liberal racial attitudes among men and women who became adults between 1960 and 1990.[9]

Progressives who maintain that we are all racists in spite of these studies attack the validity of the studies. Because the studies rely on the self-evaluations of the people being polled, critics in effect characterize persons who report nonprejudiced personal beliefs as either hypocritical, sub rosa racists or unconscious, aversive racists.

## HYPOCRITICAL RACISTS

In *Black Innocence and the White Jury*, Sheri Lynn Johnson, a noted expert on racism in criminal justice, sees hypocrisy playing a big role in the self-evaluations that seem to indicate growing racial tolerance.[10] According to Johnson, "[A]ny encouragement that might be drawn from the initial decrease in extreme negative stereotypes must be qualified by the likelihood that newer data reflect some fading of stereotypes—but also some faking."[11] From this viewpoint, prejudice has not decreased nearly as much as it seems; it has just become less socially acceptable. Thus, merely to appear socially desirable, many survey respondents profess racial liberalism. Although Johnson does not give a concrete estimate of how much "faking" the newer data reflect, she does suggest that "it now may be quite common to underreport prejudiced attitudes" by faking racial tolerance.[12]

To support the hypocrisy interpretation, Johnson points to the findings of an experiment in which White subjects were asked to report their responses to Blacks under a normal (control) condition and under a "bogus pipeline" condition. In the pipeline condition, a researcher wires his subjects to a machine that the subjects believe will give him an accurate physiological measure of (i.e., a pipeline to) their automatic or "covert" reactions.[13] The researchers then asked these subjects to estimate what the machine was telling the experimenter about their uncontrolled responses to Blacks, as the experimenter asked them to rate Blacks on various personality traits, such as ignorance, stupidity, honesty, and sensitivity. Researchers assumed that these estimations would correspond to the subjects' "honest" beliefs about Blacks. Subjects' estimates of their uncontrolled responses to Blacks in the pipeline condition were significantly more negative than the responses to Blacks reported by subjects who did not believe that their uncontrolled responses were being monitored.[14]

Johnson characterizes these automatic, uncontrolled physiological responses in this experiment as the subjects' "true feelings" and "pure" attitudes.[15] She interprets these findings as proof of prejudice's persistence notwithstanding survey data to the contrary. This interpretation, however, rests on a failure to distinguish between two distinct sources of negative responses to Blacks (and other marginalized social groups)—namely, stereotypes and prejudice. Once this critical distinction is understood, it becomes evident that the bogus pipeline results prove only the persistence of stereotypes, not prejudice, and therefore are perfectly consistent with the proposition that prejudice has decreased significantly over the last forty years.

Stereotypes consist of well-learned sets of associations among groups and traits established in children's memories at an early age, before they have the cognitive skills to decide rationally upon the personal acceptability of the stereotypes.[16] For example, Dr. Phyllis Katz reports a chilling case of a three-year-old child who, upon seeing a Black infant, said to her mother, "Look, Mom, a baby maid."[17] By the time the child turned three, before she had developed the cognitive ability to judge the appropriateness of the stereotypic ascription, the associational link between Black women and certain social roles was already forged in her memory.[18]

In contrast, prejudice consists of derogatory *personal beliefs*.[19] "Beliefs" are propositions that people endorse and accept as being true.[20] Thus, prejudiced personal beliefs are the endorsement or acceptance of a negative cultural stereotype.[21] That a person has a negative stereotype established in her memory does not necessarily mean that she endorses that stereotype. As Patricia Devine, a leading psychologist who has won prestigious awards for her trailblazing research in this area, points out, "Although one may have *knowledge of a stereotype*, his or her *personal beliefs* may or may not be congruent with the stereotype."[22] For example, if the three-year-old child described above grows up and decides that the stereotype of a maid is an inappropriate basis for responding to Black women, she may experience a fundamental conflict between the previously established stereotype and the more recently established non-prejudiced personal belief. In such a case, her responses to Black women and to Blacks generally will turn on whether those responses are based on the well-established stereotype or her more recently adopted nonprejudiced beliefs.

Of course, some people's stereotypes and personal beliefs overlap; that is, some people not only have knowledge of the cultural stereotypes from years of socialization, but they endorse and accept them as well. We shall refer to these individuals as *high prejudiced*.[23] However, many people have thought about the cultural stereotypes, recognized them as inappropriate bases for responding to others, and deliberately rejected them. We shall refer to these individuals as *low prejudiced*.[24] Although high- and low-prejudiced persons differ in their personal beliefs about Blacks, common socialization experiences have firmly entrenched the cultural stereotype of Blacks in the memories of both.

The failure to distinguish between stereotypes and prejudiced personal beliefs leads Johnson and other commentators to take an all-or-none approach to prejudice: if a person experiences any stereotype-congruent responses in any situation, she is prejudiced. This view fails to recognize that a change in a person's beliefs does not instantly extinguish habitual responses derived from well-learned stereotypes. Because stereotypes are established in children's memories at an early age and constantly reinforced through the mass media and other socializing agents, stereotype-congruent responses may persist long after a person has sincerely renounced prejudice. Nonprejudiced beliefs and stereotype-congruent thoughts and feelings may coexist within the same individual.[25] Dr. Thomas Pettigrew, a leading

authority on stereotypes and prejudice, has described one example of this conflict: "Many Southerners have confessed to me . . .
that even though in their minds they no longer feel prejudice
against Blacks, they still feel squeamish when they shake hands
with a Black. The feelings are left over from what they learned
in their families as children."[26]

There is strong empirical evidence that the vast majority of
low-prejudiced people realize that they are prone to stereotype-
congruent responses, that is, that their *actual* reactions to Blacks
and other socially marginalized groups sometimes conflict with
their personal standards for how they *should* respond. In one
recent study, researchers gave a sample of several hundred
White subjects (college students, very few of whom were high
prejudiced)[27] a questionnaire, the first section of which asked
them to report their personal standards for how they *should*
respond in five different situations involving Black people. For
example, one situation read as follows: "Imagine that a Black
person boarded a bus and sat next to you. You *should* feel
uncomfortable that a Black is sitting next to you."[28]

The subjects were asked to circle the number between 1
(strongly disagree) and 7 (strongly agree) that best reflected
their personal standard for how they *should* respond in each situation. The second section of the questionnaire asked the subjects to report on the 1-to-7 scale how they believed they actually *would* respond in the same five situations. Out of the 101
cases, 71 percent of the subjects reported actual *would* responses
that were more negative than their *should* responses, which
reflected their personal standards for how they should
respond.[29] Separate studies found similar should-would discrepancies in responses to homosexual men.[30] These studies also
investigated whether the subjects' personal standards (shoulds)

were well internalized (i.e., viewed by the subjects as highly important and as central to their personal identity or merely derived from society's standards). Researchers found that low-prejudiced subjects strongly internalized their personal standards, and that these subjects felt compunction (guilt and self-criticism) when they transgressed the standards.[31]

These findings, which several later studies have replicated, suggest a less-pessimistic interpretation of the bogus pipeline results than Johnson adopts. That a subject reports more negative responses about Blacks when he believes an experimenter can monitor his autonomic nervous system (or what Johnson refers to as his "true attitudes") does not prove that he is truly prejudiced or that he is faking his more positive responses on questionnaires. It may show only that he realizes, as most low-prejudiced people do, that he is prone to stereotype-congruent responses. Although he may not endorse these responses and may feel compunction about experiencing them, he may believe that the pipeline will detect their presence. In other situations, however, such as responding to a questionnaire, the low-prejudiced person may inhibit his stereotype-congruent responses and replace them with responses based on his nonprejudiced personal standards. A model of prejudice that recognizes the distinction between stereotypes and prejudiced personal beliefs—a model we shall call the "dissociation model"—points to the possibility of inhibiting and replacing stereotype-congruent responses with nonprejudiced responses derived from nonprejudiced personal beliefs. If nonprejudiced personal beliefs can counteract stereotypes in this way, perhaps there is hope for combating the influence of ubiquitous derogatory stereotypes.

Responses derived from nonprejudiced personal beliefs can inhibit and replace responses derived from stereotypes. Low-

and high-prejudiced people, as discussed below, are equally prone to stereotype-congruent responses when they cannot consciously monitor their responses to questions. However, low- and high-prejudiced people have given very different responses when they have had to think consciously about what their responses imply about their self-image. For example, one study asked subjects to list all of their own thoughts (e.g., beliefs, feelings, expectancies) about Blacks under strictly anonymous conditions, thus eliminating any reason to manufacture "correct" responses.[32] The high-prejudiced subjects listed primarily negative stereotypical thoughts about Blacks and were inclined to stereotype. In contrast, the low-prejudiced subjects wrote few pejorative thoughts; they reported beliefs that contradicted the stereotype and emphasized the importance of racial equality.[33] These results make intuitive sense. For low-prejudiced people, writing stereotype-congruent thoughts would contradict their personal beliefs and threaten their non-prejudiced identity. But because beliefs of high-prejudiced people overlap with stereotypes, conscious reflection should not inhibit their stereotype-congruent responses. Thus, if personal beliefs *really matter*, if they can counteract the stereotype-congruent responses to which research shows high- and low-prejudiced people are equally prone, then the thoughts that low-prejudiced subjects anonymously list about Blacks should be very different from the thoughts anonymously listed by high-prejudiced subjects.

The findings of this thought-listing study, which are strongly confirmed and extended by other research discussed below, reveal that much more than semantics is at stake in the distinction between stereotypes and prejudice. For inasmuch as negative stereotypes and personal beliefs diverge, as they do in low-prejudiced people, they imply different responses to stereotyped groups. This insight enables us to investigate the interplay between the two conceptually distinct sets of responses, and to develop strategies for activating the responses based on non-prejudiced personal beliefs and inhibiting the stereotype-congruent responses. Before elaborating a framework for working out the full implications of the interplay between stereotypes and nonprejudiced personal beliefs, we must consider the other major attack on the validity and efficacy of nonprejudiced personal beliefs: aversive racism.

## AVERSIVE RACISTS

A dominant model of prejudice is the theory of aversive racism. Whereas the hypocritical racist model posits that people who express nonprejudiced personal beliefs are manipulating their self-presentation to appear more socially desirable, the aversive racist model holds that ostensibly nonprejudiced people are not so much deceiving others as fooling themselves. The two models are not mutually exclusive, but complementary. Progressive critics freely switch from one to the other[34] in dismissing the validity of people's racially liberal self-descriptions and nonprejudiced personal beliefs.

The theory of aversive racism begins with the proposition that most Americans are highly committed to egalitarian values. Therefore, they desire to maintain an egalitarian, nonprejudiced self-image. This desire causes them to express nonprejudiced personal beliefs.[35] Such professed nonprejudiced beliefs are not to be confused with genuine—that is, well-internalized—nonprejudiced beliefs, for deep down "aversive racist[s] believe[] in White superiority"[36] and "do not want to associate with Blacks."[37] Desperately clinging to their egalitarian, nonprejudiced values and self-image, aversive racists repress their negative feelings and beliefs about Blacks. These repressed anti-Black beliefs have been called "hidden prejudice."[38] Because aversive racists do not recognize their anti-Black attitudes, the prospects for prejudice reduction are particularly dim. Here the pessimism of the aversive racism model asserts itself. Writing from this perspective, one progressive writer observes, "It is difficult to change an attitude that is unacknowledged. Thus, 'like a virus that mutates into new forms, old-fashioned prejudice seems to have evolved into a new type that is, at least temporarily, resistant to traditional . . . remedies.'"[39]

Proof of aversive racism, some believe, lies in the discrepancy between responses to Blacks that are consciously monitored and those that are not consciously monitored. Whenever aversive racists consciously monitor their responses to Blacks, they do not discriminate against them since discrimination would undermine their egalitarian self-images. For example, verbal responses to questionnaires designed to measure racial prejudice can be monitored consciously by the respondents and therefore cannot identify aversive racists.[40] More generally, if the situation clearly calls for a nonprejudiced response or if a *nonracial* justification or rationalization for engaging in a prejudiced response cannot be generated, the response will be positive because it cannot escape being consciously monitored.

In contrast, when the situation is normatively ambiguous, or when a *nonrace-related* justification is handy, the covert anti-Black attitudes and beliefs of aversive racists find expression in racial discrimination. For example, White research subjects led to believe that a person was in distress helped Black victims as often as White victims when there was no ostensible justification for a failure to help.[41] However, if the subjects knew that someone was available to help, they "helped Black victims much less frequently than they helped White victims (38% vs. 75%)."[42] According to proponents of the aversive racism model, the availability of other potential rescuers provided subjects with a convenient nonracial excuse for not helping the Black victims. This interpretation of the helping behavior study carries very discouraging implications for racially fair dispute resolution. For in courtrooms, for example, finding a nonracial reason to discriminate against a Black litigant is especially easy to do—one simply gives more weight to the evidence favoring the opposing litigant.

The aversive racism model, however, is empirically and conceptually incomplete. One empirical problem with the model stems from its assumption that aversive racists—who, according to commentators, now include most Americans—are not aware of their conflicting reactions to Blacks; their anti-Black thoughts and feelings are supposedly excluded from consciousness. If this assumption were accurate, most survey respondents would not report discrepancies between their standards for how they should respond to Blacks and how they actually would respond, since they are unaware. Yet the vast majority of subjects in several studies recognized and acknowledged that they sometimes experience such discrepancies. Thus, although the aversive racism framework may describe some White Americans, it almost certainly does not account for most.

Another empirical problem with the aversive racism theory concerns the Freudian theory of unconscious motivation to which it is often wedded.[43] Psychoanalytic theory presents real difficulties for empirical verification. A model, such as aversive racism, whose theoretical underpinnings are not empirically demonstrable demands an intellectual leap of faith that many may be unwilling to make.

The conceptual problem with the aversive racism model grows out of its tendency to conflate stereotype and prejudice. One implication of aversive racism theory—an implication explicitly embraced by some of its supporters—is that because we have all been influenced by derogatory information about Blacks, we are all racists. This conclusion fails to fully consider that people do not always endorse the knowledge structures that socialization has established in their memories. For example, although socializing forces undoubtedly have entrenched the cultural stereotype of women in the memory of feminists as well as every other American, feminists could be called "sexists" only in a Pickwickian sense. One reason it seems so anomalous to apply the value-laden term "sexist" to feminists is because feminists have both renounced the cultural stereotype about women and developed egalitarian personal beliefs about women. Thus, feminists have two distinct and conflicting cognitive structures concerning women: the cultural stereotype and their egalitarian personal beliefs. Similarly, low-prejudiced people have two conflicting cognitive structures concerning Blacks: the Black cultural stereotype and their nonprejudiced personal beliefs. Calling feminists "sexists" and low-prejudiced persons "racists" identifies them more with the well-learned cultural stereotype than with their personal beliefs, and implies that the stereotype is somehow the more compelling of the two knowledge structures.

What we need is a new, empirically demonstrated, conceptually coherent theory of prejudice. The theory must show how unconscious discrimination drives the social judgments of all Americans. Having diagnosed the ulcer of ubiquitous unconscious bias, it will not do simply to roughly finger it with bitter invective. The theory must also point to proven strategies for combating the unconscious discrimination tendencies that lurk in us all.

### Proving Ubiquitous Unconscious Bias

[G]iven a sensory input with equally good fit to two nonoverlapping categories, the more accessible of the two categories would "capture" the input.
—Jerome S. Bruner, *Psychological Review* 123 (1957)

It is widely believed that our judgments and memories of others turn on whatever information about them has been made available to us. But if information alone were sufficient to determine our social judgments, then reasonable people who are exposed to the same information about someone should form the same judgments. Yet, people often form different judgments and recollect different facts, even when exposed to the same information. Thus, in addition to information from the environmental and social context, the perceiver's cognitive structures and processes must also determine his or her social judgments. The following question therefore arises: What are these processes and what implications do they carry for social judgments of Blacks and other stereotyped groups?

Social cognition researchers conceptualize the process that underlies the perception of persons as a categorization process.[44] We must categorize to make sense of the "buzzing, blooming confusion" of stimuli that bombard us every waking moment. Attempting to deal with every event on an individual basis would rapidly overwhelm our brain's limited capacity to process information. Thus, a person who is asked to judge another's behavior must first take whatever information she receives about the other's behavior and interpret, or *encode*, this behavior by assigning it to a category. Social and personal categories include information about social groups (e.g., Blacks, women, gays, and lesbians), social roles and occupations (e.g., spouses, maids, police officers), traits and behaviors (e.g., hostile, crime prone, patriotic, and intelligent), and social types (e.g., intellectuals, social activists, and rednecks).[45] Once the behavior is assigned to one of these categories, it is stored in memory, from which it subsequently can be retrieved to make further inferences and predictions about the person.

When individuals must judge another's behavior, however, they are unlikely to perform an exhaustive search of memory for all potentially relevant categories, compare the behavior to each such category, and then characterize the behavior in terms of the category with the best "fit." Rather, they are likely to base their judgment on the category that happens to be the most readily *accessible* at the time the information is received.[46] Consider the following example:

> [J]ust after viewing an extremely violent film in which a heartless mugger preys upon innocent travelers of the city streets, a moviegoer would have a greater than usual tendency to perceive the behavior of a stranger who bumps into him or her as reflecting hostility or aggressiveness. Alternatively, after viewing a comedy featuring the inept Inspector Clouseau, the moviegoer might be more likely to perceive the identical social interaction in terms of the stranger's clumsiness. In each example, the film preceding the interaction "primed" particular cognitive categories that subsequently influenced the interpretation of the incident.[47]

Numerous studies confirm this intuitive account of the tendency of the mind to form social judgments by having incoming information about people "captured" by the mental category that is most accessible because of "priming." One classic study posited that unobtrusively exposing subjects to certain personality trait terms in one exercise would activate, or *prime*, the categories to which these terms referred, making it more likely the subjects would use the categories to characterize a person in an unrelated context.[48] To test this hypothesis, subjects were asked to perform a complex cognitive task that momentarily exposed them to several trait terms.[49] Later, in what ostensibly was an unrelated experiment on reading comprehension, the subjects read a paragraph about a target person, which was ambiguous as to his likability.[50] After reading the passage, subjects characterized the target person in their own words. As predicted, subjects who were unobtrusively exposed to favorable trait terms tended to use those terms or their synonyms in characterizing the target, while subjects exposed to unfavorable terms tended to use those terms or their synonyms in their characterizations. In contrast, control subjects that researchers exposed to trait terms that were not applicable to interpreting the target's behavior did not vary systematically in their characterizations.[51]

These results carry enormous implications for judgments and evaluations of stereotyped groups. If cues of group membership such as race serve to prime trait categories such as hostility, people will systematically view behaviors by members of certain racial groups (e.g., Blacks) as more menacing than the *same* behaviors by members of other racial groups (e.g., Whites). Thus, Whites will interpret the same ambiguous shove as hostile or violent when an actor is Black, and as "playing around" or "dramatizing" when the actor is White.[52] Category accessibility best explains this differential perception of violence as a function of the protagonist's race: the presence of the Black actor primed the stereotype of Blacks, and since the stereotype associates Blacks with violence, the violent-behavior category was more accessible when interpreting behavioral information about Blacks than Whites.[53] These findings have been replicated in studies of schoolchildren.[54] Both Black and White children rated ambiguously aggressive behaviors (e.g., bumping in the hallway) of Black actors as being more mean or threatening than the same behaviors of White actors.

Although race clearly influences category accessibility, it remains unclear whether the influence is unconscious or conscious. It is possible that upon noticing the racial identity of the Black protagonist, the observers of the ambiguous shove (or some percentage of them) formed a conscious expectation for instances of trait categories stereotypically associated with Blacks (e.g., hostile, prone to violence). Indeed, research indicates that expecting to see an instance of a trait category increases the likelihood that a person will process ambiguous information by putting it into that category.[55]

On the other hand, the observers (or some percentage of them) could have been sincerely nonprejudiced and refrained from consciously forming any race-based expectation of hostility, yet the mere presence of the Black protagonist may have automatically (i.e., unconsciously) activated the Black stereotype, including the hostility trait category that figures so prominently in that stereotype.[56] Thus, the subjects could have sincerely renounced racial prejudice and still unconsciously practiced discrimination against the Black actor. To understand how a knowledge structure such as a stereotype can operate outside a person's awareness and determine his or her responses to others, it is necessary to understand the distinction between habits and decisions, a distinction cognitive psychologists characterize in terms of *automatic* versus *controlled* processes. Since this distinction also sheds light on the interplay of stereotypes and personal beliefs in responses to members of stereotyped groups, and ultimately points to strategies for discrimination reduction, we shall discuss it in detail.

A habit is "an action that has been done many times and has become automatic. That is, it is done without conscious thought."[57] In contrast, a decision to take or not to take an action involves conscious thought.[58] The distinction between habit and conscious decision is one of the oldest concepts in psychology. In his *Principles of Psychology* (1890), William James described the origins and consequences of habit as follows: "[A]ny sequence of mental action which has been frequently repeated tends to perpetuate itself; so that we find ourselves automatically prompted to *think*, *feel*, or *do* what we have been before accustomed to think, feel, or do, under like circumstances, without any consciously formed *purpose*, or anticipation of results."[59] James concluded that it is necessary to free limited consciousness from the many mundane requirements of life by removing frequently used or habitual mental sequences from conscious awareness.[60]

The current model of habits and decisions employed by cognitive psychologists is not appreciably different from that outlined by James over a century ago, except that the current model expresses the distinction in terms of *automatic* versus *controlled* processes.[61] According to cognitive psychologists, "Habits are the results of automatic cognitive processes."[62] As Patricia G. Devine points out, "Automatic processes involve the unintentional or spontaneous activation of some well-learned set of associations or responses that have been developed through repeated activation in memory."[63] Controlled processes, on the other hand, "are intentional and require the active attention of the individual."[64] Learning to drive a car provides a useful illustration of this distinction. When you first get behind the wheel, virtually every maneuver is a controlled response. Deciding when and how to apply your foot to the pedals as you turn the steering wheel or manually shift gears demands concentration and effort. After enough practice, however, these maneuvers become automatic. You can accelerate, brake, and steer while contemplating health care reform or talking to a traveling companion. The well-learned motor responses occur without conscious effort.

A critical characteristic of habits or automatic processes is that they can operate independently of conscious decisions to break with old patterns of responses and adopt new ones.[65] Thus, attitudes and beliefs can change without a corresponding change in established habits, resulting in a conflict between currently endorsed responses and old habitual responses.[66] Anyone who has ever tried to break a bad habit knows the persistence of habitual responses in the face of decisions to adopt new ones.

Applied to the relationship between stereotypes and personal beliefs, the habit-decision/automatic-controlled processes distinction provides critical theoretical support for understanding the *more* and *less* conscious aspects of responses to Blacks (and members of other stereotyped groups). As discussed earlier, the Black stereotype is established in children's memories before children develop the cognitive ability to critically evaluate and decide on the stereotype's acceptability. Further, the social environment,[67] including the mass media,[68] incessantly reactivates this stereotype. Thus the stereotype is an ingrained set of associations (i.e., a habit) that involves automatic processes. Nonprejudiced personal beliefs, on the other hand, are necessarily newer cognitive structures that result from a low-prejudiced person's conscious decision that stereotype-based responses to Blacks are unacceptable.[69]

It follows that these decisions to renounce the already-established stereotype do not come to mind (i.e., are not reactivated) nearly as frequently as the social environment automatically activates the stereotype. Because the stereotype has a longer history and greater frequency of activation than the more recently acquired personal beliefs, even people with well-internalized nonprejudiced beliefs are likely to experience a fundamental conflict between the stereotype and their personal beliefs. The discrepancies that most low-prejudiced subjects report between how they believe they *should* respond and how they actually *would* respond in contact situations with Blacks (as well as gays) reflect this conflict. That these subjects also report feeling compunction (i.e., guilt and self-criticism) as a result of these discrepancies implies that they regard the stereotypecongruent responses as essentially a bad habit.

This analysis assumes that just as habitual responses (like putting on a seat belt) may be triggered automatically by the presence of relevant environmental cues (like sitting in a car),[70] stereotype-congruent responses may be triggered automatically by a group membership cue such as a person's racial identity (or its symbolic equivalent). This means that for a person who rejects the stereotype to avoid stereotype-congruent responses to Blacks (i.e., to avoid falling into a bad habit), she must intentionally inhibit the automatically activated stereotype and activate her newer personal belief structure. As Devine points out, "Such inhibition and initiation of new responses involves controlled processes."[71] That is, "nonprejudiced responses take intention, attention, and effort."[72]

A particularly illuminating implication of this model is that unless a low-prejudiced person consciously monitors and inhibits the activation of a stereotype in the presence of a member (or symbolic equivalent) of a stereotyped group, she may unintentionally fall into the discrimination habit. For example, the Whites in the previously researched study who interpreted the same ambiguous shove as hostile when the actor was Black and as innocuous when the actor was White could have had well-internalized nonprejudiced beliefs. However, they may not have consciously monitored the automatic activation of the Black stereotype. Because Blacks are stereotypically viewed as hostile, activation of the stereotype would have primed the hostility category, making it more accessible for social judgments about the Black actor. Since the Black stereotype is automatically activated, it could have biased subjects' judgment of the Black actor unconsciously.

One strength of this model, then, is that it explains how even people with well-internalized nonprejudiced standards are capable of unconscious discrimination against Blacks. One extraordinarily revealing experiment examined how automatic processes affected responses to members of a stereotyped group. The experiment involved presenting stereotype-related information to persons below their perceptual threshold, so that subjects could not consciously process the information. Thus, any effects of such subliminally presented information on subsequent social judgments would necessarily result from automatic processes. The experiment found that the effects of automatic stereotype activation are equally strong and inescapable for high- and low-prejudiced subjects.

In the study, both high- and low-prejudiced subjects performed a task that exposed them to either a low concentration

(20 percent of a hundred-word list) or a high concentration (80 percent of a hundred-word list) of Black stereotype labels (e.g., afro, lazy, musical, athletic, poor, etc.) in a manner determined to be effectively outside their conscious awareness.[73] For example, to prevent subjects from having conscious access to the labels, the labels were presented very rapidly (within a time frame of eighty milliseconds) and were followed immediately by a mask (i.e., a series of jumbled letters). None of these labels, or "primes," were related to hostility.[74] In an ostensibly unrelated second experiment, subjects read a behavioral description of a person named Donald, whose race was not specified and who was engaging in a series of ambiguously hostile behaviors. For example, Donald demands his money back from a store clerk immediately after a purchase and refuses to pay his rent until his apartment is repainted. Devine found that both high- and low-prejudiced subjects' ratings of the target's hostility were significantly higher (i.e., indicated more hostility) when subliminally exposed to a high, rather than a low, concentration of Black-stereotype labels.[75]

These findings demonstrate that well-learned sets of associations like stereotypes can be activated automatically in perceivers' memories and can affect subsequent social judgments. The effects of automatic stereotype priming on subjects' evaluation of the target person's hostility are especially revealing because no hostility-related traits were used as primes. Thus, it seems that the Black stereotype must be constructed cognitively in such a way that activating one component of the stereotype simultaneously primes or activates the remaining closely associated components as well.[76] These findings also suggest that even low-prejudiced subjects who have well-internalized, nonprejudiced beliefs about Blacks have cognitive structures (i.e., stereotypes) that automatically produce stereotype-congruent evaluations of ambiguous behaviors when subjects cannot monitor stereotype activation consciously.

In this sense, we are all prone to stereotype-congruent or prejudice-like responses to Blacks and other stereotyped groups. However, the research demonstrating disassociation of stereotypes and personal beliefs in low-prejudiced people argues against the conclusion that "we are all racists." It is more accurate and useful to say that "we are all creatures of habit."

## Combating Unconscious Discrimination in the Courtroom

Perhaps the most important strength of the dissociation model of automatic and controlled processes outlined here is that it suggests a strategy for resisting unconscious discrimination. Thus far, the model has focused on how people who are firmly committed to their low-prejudiced beliefs[77] remain prone to automatic activation of stereotypes. For such individuals to resist falling into the discrimination habit, they repeatedly recall their personal beliefs so that their social judgments become based on these beliefs rather than on the stereotypes. Reminding decision makers of their personal beliefs, therefore, may help them to resist falling unconsciously into the discrimination habit. Is there any proof that this approach works?

### EMPIRICAL SUPPORT FOR THE STRATEGY

Considerable empirical evidence shows that responses based on automatic processes can be inhibited and replaced by responses based on controlled processes.[78] Focusing on the effect of gender stereotypes on memory, for example, psychologists have found that when gender was not brought situationally to subjects' attention, or made "salient,"[79] subjects' descriptions of self and others reflected more traditional views of gender-linked attributes.[80] Under such conditions, traditional gender stereotypes, with their longer history and greater frequency of activation, are activated automatically and influence recall.[81] When gender was brought to the subjects' attention or made salient, however, they apparently inhibited the traditional stereotype, and descriptions were more consistent with their more recently developed, modern views of gender-linked attributes.[82] In other words, when the subjects were reminded of gender, they checked their stereotype-congruent responses more assiduously than when gender was less salient.

This approach also explains the proclivity of White rescuers to help White but not Black victims in distress. Recall that White research subjects led to believe that a person was in distress helped Black victims as often as White victims when there was no ostensible justification for a failure to help. On the other hand, if the subjects knew of the availability of another who might help, they "helped Black victims much less frequently than they helped White victims." According to the dissociation model, when the subjects believed they were the only potential rescuer, they were required consciously to think about what their responses to the Black victim's call of distress implied about their nonprejudiced self-conceptions. When the conflict between their nonprejudiced personal beliefs and the stereotype of Blacks is made salient in this way, the dissociation model predicts that low-prejudiced persons are likely to resolve the conflict by inhibiting their prejudice-like responses and reaffirming their nonprejudiced self-conceptions. On the other hand, when the subjects believed that there were others who might help, the stereotype-personal belief conflict was less salient and the low-prejudiced subjects were therefore less likely to monitor and inhibit responses based on the negative Black stereotype.[83]

### A NARRATIVE OF HOPE

"YOU'RE ALL PREJUDICED" DARROW TELLS JURY
—Headline, *Detroit Free Press*, May 12, 1926

Clarence Darrow, one of the most famous lawyers in American history, directly challenged jurors to confront their own prejudices in a dramatic murder trial early in this century. The case involved a Black family who moved into a middle-class White neighborhood in Detroit in 1925. When Dr. Ossian H. Sweet and his wife moved into the neighborhood with their baby daughter, they knew that other Blacks who had bought homes in White neighborhoods had been forced to move by "Improvement Associations." Accordingly, Dr. Sweet brought along his brothers, several friends, and an ample supply of guns and ammunition. Two nights after his arrival, a large White crowd, estimated at several hundred, gathered around the house and began throwing stones at the house amid cries of "Niggers." Although police officers were present to maintain order, they stood idly by as the barrage of rocks increased. Seeing a big stone crash through an upstairs window and watching the crowd make a sudden movement, both Sweet and his younger brother, Henry, fired a warning shot over the heads of the boisterous mob. One of the mob's members was killed.

Everyone in the house—eleven Black people—was arrested and charged with first-degree murder. The NAACP asked Darrow to come out of retirement to defend the Sweets. Darrow agreed. In his summation to the jury, Darrow challenged them to confront their own racial biases directly:

> The prosecutor says that this isn't a race question; it is a murder case. He says, "We don't want any prejudice; we don't want the other side to have any. Race and color have nothing to do with the case. This is a case of murder."
>
> . . . .
>
> I insist that there is nothing but prejudice in this case; that if it was reversed and 11 Whites had shot and killed a Black while protecting their home and lives against a mob of Blacks, nobody would have dreamed of having them indicted. They would have been given medals instead.
>
> . . . .
>
> I haven't any doubt but that every one of you is prejudiced against colored people. I want you to guard against it. I want you to do all you can to be fair in this case, and I believe you will.
>
> . . . .
>
> You need not tell me you are not prejudiced. I know better. We are not very much but a bundle of prejudices anyhow. We are prejudiced against other people's color. Prejudiced against other men's religions; prejudiced against other people's politics. Prejudiced against people's looks. Prejudiced about the way they dress. We are full of prejudices.
>
> . . . .
>
> Here were eleven colored men, penned up in the house. Put yourselves in their place. Make yourselves colored for a little while. It won't hurt, you can wash it off. They can't, but you can.
>
> . . . .
>
> Suppose you were Black. Do you think you would forget it even in your dreams? Or would you have Black dreams?

Suppose you had to watch every point of contact with your neighbor and remember your color, and you knew your children were growing up under this handicap. Do you suppose you would think of anything else?

. . . .

Supposing you had your choice, right here this minute, would you rather lose your eyesight or become colored? Would you rather lose your hearing or be a Negro? Would you rather go out there on the street and have your leg cut off by a streetcar, or have a Black skin?

. . . .

All I hope for, gentlemen of the jury, is that you are strong enough, and honest enough, and decent enough to lay your prejudice aside in this case and decide it as you ought to.[84]

The jury returned a not guilty verdict for Henry Sweet, and the prosecution decided not to proceed further against any of the remaining defendants.

Dr. Sweet's case provides a compelling narrative of hope and redemption that stands in marked contrast to the pessimism of many current discussions of prejudice in the courtroom. Clarence Darrow, in the heyday of Jim Crow, successfully urged a jury of all White males to resist succumbing to their discriminatory impulses in judging the reasonableness of a Black man's use of lethal force against a White man. Darrow's feat was especially remarkable because it required Darrow to combat the influence of both stereotypes and prejudice on the fact finders. In the 1920s, just as today, American culture was replete with derogatory images of Blacks. Thus, negative Black stereotypes that could be triggered automatically by the presence of a Black person were well established in the fact finders' memories.

Moreover, the percentage of Whites who accepted or endorsed the prevailing Black stereotypes was much greater in the past than it is today. Many of Dr. Sweet's jurors, therefore, probably also formed a conscious expectation for instances of trait categories stereotypically associated with Blacks (e.g., D. W. Griffith's popular and celebrated 1915 film, *Birth of a Nation*, presented a Ku Klux Klan view of Blacks as lawless savages). Because automatic (stereotype-driven) and controlled (prejudice-driven) processes can operate simultaneously on the same underlying categories,[85] the two processes likely were mutually reinforcing in many of these jurors; that is, both processes combined additively to make the underlying negative categories about Blacks more accessible. Confronting fact finders whose personal beliefs and stereotypes about Blacks overlapped, Darrow's strategy was based on the assumption that even high-prejudiced persons personally endorse general egalitarian beliefs. Dr. Sweet's life hinged on whether the jurors— prompted by Darrow's race-conscious appeals—could resist their discriminatory impulses and respond to Dr. Sweet on the basis of their egalitarian ideals.[86] Fortunately for Dr. Sweet and those of us who find relief from despair in what his case says about the capacity of jurors to resist even their most entrenched biases, the jury responded to Darrow's plea by activating their egalitarian responses and checking their prejudiced and stereotype-congruent ones.

Today, although more people espouse nonprejudiced personal beliefs than in Darrow's time, the Black stereotype is probably no less entrenched in the memories of Americans than in Darrow's day. Indeed, with the advent of an omnipresent mass media and its incessant manipulation of stereotypes, it may be more entrenched. Thus, habitual stereotype-congruent responses to Blacks, even by sincerely racially liberal Whites, may distort social judgments about Blacks as much in contemporary America as in the America Darrow knew. If so, these distorted judgments are more insidious than before because they result from automatic processes, which often (but not necessarily always) escape conscious detection. Nevertheless, Darrow's strategy of explicitly engaging our egalitarian responses and urging us consciously to substitute them for our more habitual responses squares with modern empirical research on discrimination-reduction techniques. As the recent research in social cognition demonstrates, avoiding stereotype-congruent responses requires conscious effort by the decision maker.

A more recent criminal trial, the celebrated New York subway vigilante case of *People v. Goetz*, described in the Introduction, is an example of a case in which the failure to give direct and explicit consideration to racial factors may have resulted in less fair deliberations by the decision makers. Recall that the defendant, Bernhard Goetz, successfully claimed that his shooting of four Black teenagers after one of them requested five dollars was justified as an act of self-defense. George Fletcher, a legal theorist who witnessed the entire trial, identified numerous unmistakable instances of the defense "indirectly and covertly . . . play[ing] on the racial factor."[87] For example, the defense "relentlessly attack[ed]" the Black victims as "savages," "vultures," the "predators" on society, and the "gang of four."[88] According to the theory of stereotypes developed earlier, the use of such racial imagery[89] automatically activates and reactivates the Black stereotype. This activation renders negative thoughts and *feelings*[90] associated with that stereotype acutely accessible for social judgments about the Black victims. The decision makers may not experience these judgments as stemming from their knowledge of the Black stereotype, but instead as rational, evenhanded evaluations of objective reality. The only way to combat the effect of covert appeals to racial imagery may be to challenge explicitly the fact finders to monitor consciously their responses to avoid unconscious stereotyping. In considering the impact on the jury of the defense's use of racial imagery, Fletcher reaches conclusions about the need to openly address the racial factor that are consistent with this analysis:

> In the end, Slotnick's [Goetz's attorney] covert appeal to racial fear may have had more impact on the jury precisely because it remained hidden behind innuendo and suggestion. It spoke to that side of the jurors' personality that they could not confront directly. Paradoxically, Slotnick may have gained more from not [explicitly playing on the racial factor] than from bringing the racial issue out into the open. Openly talking about racial fear in the courtroom might have helped the jury to deal more rationally with their own racial biases.[91]

To combat Slotnick's covert appeal to racial fear and help jurors activate their nonprejudiced personal beliefs, the prosecution in Goetz might have taken a cue from Darrow and included in its closing argument the following Patricia Williams story, which, "with minor character alterations, is excerpted from Goetz's videotaped confession."[92]

> A lone Black man was riding in an elevator in a busy downtown department store. The elevator stopped on the third floor, and a crowd of noisy White high school students got on. The Black man took out a gun, shot as many of them as he could, before the doors opened on the first floor and the rest fled for their lives. The Black man later explained to the police that he could tell from the "body language" of the stu-

dents, from their "shiny eyes and big smiles," that they wanted to "play with him, like a cat plays with a mouse." Furthermore, the Black man explained, one of the youths had tried to panhandle money from him and another asked him, "How are you?"

"That's a meaningless thing," he said in his confession, but "in certain circumstances, that can be a real threat." He added that a similar greeting had preceded the vicious beating of his father, a Black civil rights lawyer in Mississippi, some time before. His intention, he confessed, was to murder the high school students.

Can there be any doubt that the Black gunman who put on such a defense before most White juries would end up not only *in* jail, but, to borrow an idiomatic Black expression for the correctional fate of perpetrators of particularly heinous transgressions, "they'd put him *up under* the jail."

### MAKING THE RUBBER MEET THE ROAD: A BLUEPRINT FOR FIGHTING THE UNCONSCIOUS BIAS OF JURORS

References to stereotyped groups in legal proceedings vary in both content and subtlety. The content of a group reference concerns the specific aspect of the stereotype that the reference invokes. For example, recent cases record attorneys playing on Black stereotypes. Prosecutors in one case told the jury that the Black defendant "had to play Superfly," a fictional Black criminal popularized in motion pictures.[93] In another case the prosecutor delivered a lengthy statement about the prevalence of Black crime, urging the jury to prevent this pattern of violence from reaching their city.[94] In yet another case the prosecutor announced to the jury that "Ninety percent of all murders are committed by Blacks on Blacks" and that "[i]ts [sic] time to say

'We're not going to allow this kind of conduct to go on in our city anymore.'"[95] Stereotypes of Italians,[96] and Native Americans[97] as more prone to violence and criminality than other Americans have also been tapped by prosecutors. Other cases describe attorneys invoking stereotypes of Blacks as subhuman, sexually predatory, and dishonest, to name a few.[98] As the earlier analysis revealed, playing on any particular aspect of a stereotype may activate the entire stereotype, thus distorting a wide range of social judgments about the stereotyped litigant.

The subtlety of group references ranges from blatant to covert and indirect. Although recent case law contains numerous examples of references from both ends of this continuum,[99] the dissociation model suggests that the more subtle references may be particularly pernicious because subtle references inconspicuously may activate the relevant stereotypes. This deprives jurors of the opportunity to monitor consciously their responses for convergence with their personal beliefs. Moreover, for courts concerned with policing inappropriate group references, subtle references pose special problems of identification. For example, Goetz's attorney Barry Slotnick did not explicitly mention race in his characterization of the Black youths his client shot as "savages" and "predators," but his statements arguably constituted subtle racial references.

To identify the covertly racial tenor of such statements, courts need a test of the symbolic significance that the culture attaches to them. For to the extent that certain references carry racial connotations, they constitute symbolic equivalents of members of that race and thus serve as cues that activate (often unconsciously) racial stereotypes. Thoughtful formulations of tests for identifying subtle racial symbolism have been developed, including "the cultural meaning test"[100] and "the racial imagery shield law."[101] Whatever test for identifying references a court adopts, fairness and accurate fact finding require that once the court identifies an inappropriate reference, it should give the opposing party the choice of a mistrial or corrective instructions. Given the enormous societal interest in racially fair legal proceedings, courts must follow a policy of "zero tolerance" with respect to inappropriate racial references.

*Admission of Rationality-Enhancing Group References.* The central thesis of this discussion, however, is that not all references to Blacks or other stereotyped groups are inappropriate. We therefore turn now to the critical distinction between rationality-enhancing and rationality-subverting group references. Group references that exploit, exacerbate, or play on the prevailing stereotypes that fact finders carry with them into the jury box subvert the rationality of the fact-finding process. But references that challenge the fact finders to reexamine and resist their discriminatory responses enhance the rationality of the fact-finding process. For example, referring to Blacks as animal-like or subhuman (e.g., "savages," "monsters," and "Tasmanian devils") resonates so strongly with prevailing Black stereotypes as to constitute rationality-subverting racial references. In contrast, Darrow's plea for jurors consciously to monitor and resist their anti-Black prejudices and stereotypes is an example of rationality-enhancing uses of group references.

Courts should recognize and apply this distinction as follows. Once a court identifies a group reference made by one litigant's counsel,[102] it should give the opposing side the choice of a mistrial or corrective instructions. This general proscription of group references should be subject to very limited exceptions.[103]

One such exception would be that the reference enhances rationality, in that it challenges fact finders to monitor and inhibit their stereotype-congruent responses.[104] To fall under this exception, the attorney making or seeking to make the reference in litigation would have to represent the interests of the member of that group and hold a good faith belief in the rationality-enhancing value of the reference. Inasmuch as courts seek to protect the truth-seeking function of the trial process, they should maintain the same goal in cases involving litigants from other stereotyped groups.

Especially sensitive are those cases in which an attorney representing a member of a stereotyped group makes an ostensibly derogatory reference to that group. The attorney may claim that such a reference actually helps fact finders resist prejudice-like responses when making judgments about the group member whom she represents. For example, on one level Darrow's statement that the White jurors would rather lose their eyesight and have their legs cut off by a streetcar than have Black skin makes a very invidious statement about the negative social value of his client's racial identity. (Today White college students regularly report that if they were suddenly to become outwardly Black while they inwardly remain who they were, reasonable compensation would be one million dollars a year for life!)[105] On another level, however, it was clear from the context in which Darrow used these ostensibly invidious racial references that they actually constituted an appeal to the jurors to rise above their prejudices on that occasion.

Similarly, in the movie *Philadelphia*, the attorney's use of the epithets associated with gay men—"faggot," "fairy," "booty snatcher," "rump-roaster"—were calculated to challenge the fact finders to confront and inhibit their habitual stereotype-congruent responses to gays, not to encourage such responses. Not mentioning race or sexual orientation at all when cues that automatically trigger the stereotypes associated with these characteristics abound promotes unconscious discrimination against members of these stereotyped groups. To control a bad habit, a person first must recall it consciously, and then intentionally inhibit it as he or she responds in ways consistent with his or her personally-endorsed beliefs and attitudes

*Timing of Rationality-Enhancing Group References.* Assuming that an attorney representing a member of a stereotyped group seeks to make rationality-enhancing group references for her client, what is the best setting for such references? Salutary group references may be made in a variety of settings, including *voir dire*, opening statements, presentation of the case in chief, closing arguments, jury instructions, and jury deliberations. All these settings present opportunities for legal actors to encourage prospective or sitting fact finders to guard against their prejudice-like responses. *Voir dire*, for example, may present an excellent opportunity to search not only for avowedly prejudiced venire persons, but also to signal to prospective jurors the importance of consciously monitoring their habitual responses to the stereotyped litigant.

Another favorable setting for rationality-enhancing group references may be during opening statements. A striking illustration of both a lawyer's efforts to activate a jury's nonprejudiced impulses in this setting, and a court's misguided application of color-blind formalism to his efforts, comes from a tort case pitting a pharmaceutical company against a low-income Black infant and her mother.[106] The mother and child sought damages for serious injuries the child suffered from using the pharmaceutical company's allegedly defective drug. In his opening statement to a mostly White jury, plaintiffs' counsel characterized the case as "a test of our judicial system to see if a child who is at the lower end of our society . . . can come before a jury and receive fair and just compensation for [her] injuries." He then directly addressed the racial dimension of the case:

> [W]e were concerned about the effect of having Black people come to an area where there are not many Black people and expecting to get justice from a jury which is mostly White people. We decided to confront this issue and we asked you the questions this morning, and we were really pleased with the responses that we got and we think that this is an impartial jury and everyone here has sworn that they will try this case not on the basis of passions, or prejudice, or economic basis, but on the basis of the facts and the law.[107]

Criticizing counsel's comments, the Third Circuit warned that "the remarks should not be repeated in the opening statement at the retrial." According to the court, the counsel's remarks were "beyond the realm of appropriate advocacy. . . . '[T]here must be limits to pleas of pure passion and there must be restraints against blatant appeals to bias and prejudice.'"[108]

In this case, the Third Circuit elided the crucial distinction between rationality-enhancing and rationality-subverting racial references. A large and compelling body of social science research—including case studies, laboratory findings in mock jury studies, and general research on racial prejudice—establishes that racial bias affects jury deliberations.[109] Perhaps the best chance for litigants like this low-income Black infant and her mother to receive a fair trial from a mostly White jury is for courts to recognize this distinction and permit rationality-enhancing racial references by a Black litigant's attorney in settings likely to maximize the salutary effects of such references.

What settings are most favorable for rationality-enhancing group references? Confronting individuals about their unconscious biases may produce different results at different stages of the litigation process. Jury studies suggest that many jurors already have made up their minds before the closing argument.[110] This suggests that perhaps *voir dire* and opening statements (and even pretrial publicity) are the most important settings for rationality-enhancing comments and confrontations. In Darrow's celebrated defense of Dr. Sweet, for example, one wonders whether, in addition to his closing argument, he also confronted the jurors' stereotypes and prejudices at earlier stages of the proceeding, and if so, whether these earlier confrontations significantly contributed to Sweet's acquittal. Perhaps the acquittal resulted from the cumulative effect of a multiplicity of factors, including Darrow's repeated salutary racial references (perhaps throughout the trial), the makeup of that particular jury and the dynamics of their group decision making, the Judge's demeanor, and the pretrial publicity and media coverage. Future research will have to try to parse out each of these variables and weigh its influence on the accuracy and fairness of the fact-finding process. This analysis has not aimed to provide a ready answer to these crucial questions, but to provide a theoretical framework for approaching them. Above all, I have attempted to establish that justice often will be better promoted if we consciously confront stereotypes than if we take a color-blind, ostrich-head-in-the-sand approach.

# CONCLUSION

Once a thief is caught, a whole string of crimes if often solved. A single psychological phenomenon can explain a host of persistent social problems. A few entrenched moral and conceptual errors can spawn a vast array of social injustices. Identifying such a phenomenon and exposing such errors has been a major objective of this book.

Our analysis of stereotypes, for example, focused on the role of the unconscious in perpetuating the Black tax, especially in the courtroom. Unconscious mental habits about stereotyped groups also help explain a variety of discriminatory behaviors in other settings, from employment discrimination to biased police enforcement. Moreover, understanding stereotypes may even provide insight into why many Blacks do poorly on standardized tests. Claude Steele, a Stanford social psychologist, has identified the phenomenon of "stereotype vulnerability" as a hidden psychological tax on Black test takers that tends to drag down their performance. Steele gave two groups of Black and White Stanford students the same test involving difficult questions from the Graduate Record Exam. Before the test, one group was told that the exercise was meant only to examine "psychological factors involved in solving verbal problems," while the other group was told that the exercise was "a genuine test of your verbal abilities and limitations." The Blacks who thought they were merely solving verbal problems scored the same as the Whites (who performed equally in both situations). But the group of Black students saddled with the extra burden of believing that the exercise measured their intelligence scored significantly below all the other students. Additional experiments show that stereotype vulnerability can drag down the performance of women who believe a given math test shows "gender differences." Steele theorizes that students' efforts not to confirm the stereotype causes them to work too quickly or inefficiently. Thus, understanding stereotypes sheds light on internal and external sources of the Black Tax.

Our analysis of stereotypes and the ubiquity of unconscious discrimination also bears on the affirmative action debate. Affirmative action is routinely characterized as a remedy for past discrimination. The experimental findings we discussed, however, demonstrate that discrimination against Blacks is prevalent here and now. Wherever social judgments about Blacks are made (including in job interviews and corporate boardrooms), there is a demonstrable tendency unconsciously to discriminate. It is pervasive present discrimination against Blacks, not past discrimination alone, that justifies affirmative efforts at inclusion.

We also discussed a popular conceptual error responsible for a long string of muddled moral and legal arguments: the notion of "rational discrimination" against Blacks. The rot at the core of this fashionable notion consists in its failure to recognize the intimate relationship between factual judgments and value judgments. Before someone acts on a factual judgment, he or she must first weigh the costs of error inherent in that judgment. Assessing the costs of error and balancing them against the benefits of "rational discrimination" ineluctably turns on value judgments. Given the costs of error in racial generalizations, the Bayesian's attempt to justify racial discrimination purely by means of arithmetic is wrongheaded.

A number of economists have recently donned the mantle of the "Intelligent Bayesian," asserting that we must tolerate a certain amount of "rational racial discrimination" in the name of market efficiency. Following the modus operandi of the Bayesians we discussed, these "rational utility maximizing" Bayesians would have us drain the discussion of racial discrimination of any normative content, focusing single-mindedly on whether such discrimination marginally promotes economic efficiency. In American history, excuses for discriminating against Blacks have often popped up like the heads of Hydra— lop off one excuse and two grow in its place. In Greek mythology, the only way to keep the Hydra-headed beast from growing back two heads for each one cut off was to cauterize each neck after severing its head. Hopefully, arguments like those developed in chapter 2 will help cauterize the "rational discrimination" neck that seems so eager to sprout more visor-wearing, number-crunching heads.

Another theme running throughout this book has been the fallacious tendency to equate the typical with the reasonable. A tangled string of crimes can be traced to this thief. Its rap sheet includes the glorification of, and unthinking obeisance to, "common sense"; the blind deference of courts to scientific orthodoxy; the theory that courts should merely observe rather than define what is "reasonable"; the belief that the law should seek only to accommodate rather than actively channel human behavior; and the hypocritical defense of our current approaches to blame and punishment. Reasonable Racists, nice Nazis, and gentlemen slavers were seen to be this fallacy's logical extensions; complacency, supine acquiescence to "authority," and avoidance of critical self-examination, its hallmarks.

As the Procrustean bed metaphor suggested, intolerance and ethnocentrism also motivate people to equate the reasonable with the typical. There is a tendency among dominant group members to attempt to flatten diversity and difference into mirror-smooth pure ego, to convert competing perspectives to allegiance to a single absolute truth that reflects only the dominant group's ideals, beliefs, and attitudes. Doubt is the devil, from this missionary mindset; blind faith, the highest virtue. Because acknowledging the validity of other points of view contradicts absolutism, inclusive movements like multiculturalism are demonized.

Doubt may give your dinner a funny taste, as they say, but it's the *absence* of doubt that goes out and kills. It is the absence of doubt that lies behind suicide bombings, slave auctions, and extermination camps. And, as we discussed in the chapter on blame and punishment, it is the absence of doubt about our ability to divine a wrongdoer's "true character" (especially a wrongdoer who was brutalized as a child, which studies show many violent criminals to have been) that lies behind our eagerness to hang, shoot, and lethally inject, at ever younger ages, in the name of justice.

One can easily grow weary—even fatalistic—contemplating the seemingly intractable problems of racial justice. Early in this now elderly century, W. E. B. Du Bois prophesied, in his monumental book, *The Souls of Black Folk*, that "[t]he problem of the twentieth century is the problem of the color-line,—the relation of the darker to the lighter races of men in Asia and Africa, in America and the islands of the sea." Over ninety years later, race continues to be an American obsession, and racial discrimination continues to pervade every aspect of the American experience. The "problem of the color-line" seems destined to plague another century.

A hopeful voice, speaking from a long-ago captivity, has echoed through these pages, however. A major premise of this book has been that there has been significant progress in race relations since the publication of *Souls of Black Folk*—the percentage of Americans who personally accept and endorse the Black stereotype has decreased. Most Americans aspire to be fair, democratic, and nonprejudiced. Nevertheless, as well-learned sets of associations, stereotypes continue to be well established in the memories of all Americans. Thus, we are all prone to falling into the discrimination habit, especially in unguarded moments. Resisting the habit requires intensive race-consciousness: relentlessly confronting and interrogating our responses to Blacks and other stereotyped groups. Race-consciousness, of course, is no panacea for the "problem of the color-line," but it must play a central role in our determined efforts to find solutions.

Racism and racial discrimination are blights on the glory of American democracy. They wither hopes, dreams, and ambitions of millions of Americans. Left unchecked, they pose the greatest internal threat to this nation's peace and prosperity. To remove them, we must first expose them, not allowing them to hide behind the calculators and pocket protectors of "rational discriminators" or beneath the robes of judges and senators. Then we must gain deeper insights into our unconscious, habitual responses to stereotyped groups, finding ways to break bad habits and answer the call of what Abraham Lincoln called the "higher angels of our nature."

# NOTES

## Notes to the Introduction

1. Jandrucko v. Colorcraft/Fuqua Corp., No. 163-20-6245 (Fla. Dep't of Lab. & Empl. Sec. Apr. 26, 1990).

2. *See, e.g.*, George P. Fletcher, *A Crime of Self-Defense: Bernhard Goetz and the Law on Trial* 206-08 (1988) (describing trial tactics used by the defense to emphasize the racial identity of the four Black alleged assailants shot by New York subway vigilante Bernhard Goetz); Sheri Lynn Johnson, "Racial Imagery in Criminal Cases," 67 *Tul. L. Rev.* 739 (1993) (exploring how the use of racial images influences criminal trials, and proposing legislation modeled after rape shield laws to curb the manipulation of racial fears and stereotypes in the courtroom).

3. 68 N.Y.2d 96, 497 N.E.2d 41, 506 N.Y.S.2d 18 (1986).

4. *Fletcher, supra* note 2, at 206 (quoting defense attorney Barry Slotnick).

5. "Latest Defense Witness in Rodney King Trial Backfires," *L.A. Sentinel,* Apr. 1, 1993, at A4. Another officer, under cross-examina-

tion by the defense, described King's beating as "a scene from a monster movie." "Beating: 'Scene from Monster Movie'," *Atlanta J. & Const.*, Mar. 11, 1992, at A3.

6. Seth Mydans, "Defense Lawyer at Beating Trial Asserts Driver Prompted Violence," *N.Y. Times*, Apr. 22, 1992, at A16.

7. For example, in the fall of 1995, 6 Philadelphia police officers pleaded guilty to corruption charges, including lying under oath and planting false evidence. "Philadelphia Feels Effects of Inquiry," *New York Times*, Mar. 24, 1996, at 35. The city settled with forty-two victims of such misconduct, paying a total of $3.5 million. In another settlement reflecting the city's concern over police corruption and racial bias, Philadelphia agreed to expand supervision of its police force. "Philadelphia Is in Accord in Police Corruption Case," *New York Times*, Sept. 5, 1996, at A14.

### Notes to Chapter 1

1. Mark Kelman, "Reasonable Evidence of Reasonableness," 17 *Critical Inquiry* 798, 801 (1991).

2. Tom W. Smith, *Ethnic Images* 9, 16 (Dec. 1990) (General Social Survey Topical Report No. 19, on file with the *Stanford Law Review*).

3. *E.g.*, Keith Harriston, "3 Cab Firms to Monitor for Bias: Suit over Shunning of Blacks Settled," *Wash. Post*, Nov. 3, 1990, at Bl; "The Jeweler's Dilemma," *New Republic*, Nov. 10, 1986, at 18; Clarence Page, "Black Youths: Buzz In or Buzz Off?" *Chi. Trib.*, Nov. 2, 1986, § 5, at 3; Sam Roberts, "Hailing a Taxi is Even Harder if You're Black," *N.Y. Times*, Dec. 10, 1987, at Bl; "Fear of Blacks, Fear of Crime," *N.Y. Times*, Dec. 28, 1986, at 10.

4. Wayne R. LaFave & Austin W. Scott, Jr., *Criminal Law* § 5.7 (2d ed. 1986). The defender must have *honestly* and *reasonably* believed that the feared attack was *imminent*, and that her response to it was both *necessary and proportional*.

In other words, valid self-defense requires that the defender honestly and reasonably believe three things: first, that the harm he inflicts on the other does not exceed the harm he spares himself(proportionality); second, that there is a high probability the other is launching an attack (imminence); and finally, that there is no less drastic way to repel the attack than to use the force he used (necessity).

5. However, in New York, for example, attempted robbery is considered a sufficiently threatening crime to warrant a response with deadly force.

6. LaFave & Scott, *supra* note 4, § 5.7(c).

7. *See, e.g.*, 2 Fowler v. Harper & Fleming James, Jr., *The Law of Torts* § 16.2 (1956).

8. This formulation is quoted in an English case, Hall v. Brooklands Auto Racing Club, [1933] 1 K.B. 205, 224, and attributed to an unnamed American author. *See also* Guido Calabresi, *Ideals, Beliefs, Attitudes, and the Law* 23 (1985).

9. Joshua Dressler, "Commentaries: When 'Heterosexual' Men Kill 'Homosexual' Men: Reflections on Provocation Law, Sexual Advances, and the 'Reasonable Man' Standard," 85 *J. Crim. L.* 726, 753 (1995).

10. Kelman, *supra* note 1, at 800.

11. Daubert v. Merrell Dow Pharmaceuticals, 113 S. Ct. 2786 (1993).

12. *Kelman, supra* note 1, at 801.

13. *Id.*

14. *See, e.g.*, George P. Fletcher, "The Theory of Criminal Negligence: A Comparative Analysis," 119 *U. Pa. L. Rev.* 401, 417-18 (1971) (arguing that the determination of whether a defendant deserves to be excused mirrors the inquiry into whether the accused is morally culpable for violating the law).

15. See Carolyn Choi, Note, "Applications of a Cultural Defense in Criminal Proceedings," 8 *Pac. Basin L.J.* 80, 83 n.37 (1990) (People v. Moua, No. 315972 (Fresno Super. Ct. 1985)).

16. People v. Wu, 286 *Cal. Rptr.* 868, 872-73 (Cal. Ct. App. 1991).

17. Frederick M. Binder, *The Color Problem in Early National America as Viewed by John Adams, Jefferson and Jackson* 48-81 (1968).

18. A psychological analogue of the internalist approach can be seen in the Rokeach confrontation technique. Rokeach's strategy was inspired by Gunner Myrdal's characterization of the American Dilemma. According to Myrdal, many White Americans who are com-

mitted to the general egalitarian tenets of the "American Creed" but who simultaneously have specific prejudiced tendencies experience an internal moral conflict. Rokeach reasoned that self-dissatisfaction arises when people are encouraged to recognize the discrepancy between their egalitarian self-conception and their prejudiced responses. This self-dissatisfaction should then motivate individuals to change the prejudiced aspects of their responses to be more in line with their egalitarian self-image. (In chapter 6 I show how a famous American lawyer employed this technique in successfully defending a Black man before an all-White jury in the heyday of Jim Crow.)

19. Melvin A. Eisenberg, *The Nature of the Common Law* 15 (1988).

20. 60 F.2d 737 (2d Cir.), *cert. denied,* 287 U.S. 662 (1932).

21. For a parallel analysis of the normative dimension of the reasonable man test in the context of the duress defense in criminal law, *see* Jody D. Armour, "Race Ipsa Loquitur: Of Reasonable Racists, Intelligent Bayesians, and Involuntary Negrophobes," 46 *Stan. L. Rev.* 781, 789-90 (1994).

### Notes to Chapter 2

1. January 17, 1994.

2. December 21, 1994.

3. Walter E. Williams, "The Intelligent Bayesian," in *The Jeweler's Dilemma, New Republic,* Nov. 10, 1986, at 18.

4. Michael Levin, Responses to Race Differences in Crime, Journal of Social Philosophy 5, 7 (Spring 1992).

5. Marc Mauer & Tracy Huling, *Young Black Americans and the Criminal Justice System: Five Years Later,* The Sentencing Project 3 (1995).

6. *Id.* at 9; see also David A. Slansky, "Cocaine, Race, and Equal Protection," 47 *Stan. L. Rev.* 1283 (1995)(discussing the disparate impact of severe crack cocaine penalties on Black vs. White crack offenders).

7. *Id.* at 14; see also Delgado, "Rodrigo's Eighth Chronicle: Black Crime, White Fears—On the Social Construction of Threat," 80 *Va. L.*

*Rev.* 503 (1994). According to the 1993 Federal Bureau of Investigation's Uniform Crime Reports (UCR), 52.6 percent of arrestees for violent crime were White and 45.7 percent were Black. Federal Bureau of Investigation, U.S. Department of Justice, Uniform Crime Reports for the United States 235 (1993). In 1994, the percentage of White arrestees for violent crime went up to 53.4 percent and the percentage of Black arrestees for violent crime declined to 44.7 percent. Federal Bureau of Investigation, U.S. Department of Justice, Uniform Crime Reports for the United States 235 (1994).

8. Mark Kelman, "Reasonable Evidence of Reasonableness," 17 *Critical Inquiry*, 798, 814 n.20 (1991).

9. *Id.*

10. According to the Uniform Crime Reports, 288,133 Blacks were arrested for violent crimes in 1994. Federal Bureau of Investigation, U.S. Department of Justice, Uniform Crime Reports for the United States 235 (1994). According to the Bureau of the Census, the total Black population in the United States in 1994 was 32,672,000 and the total Black male population was 15,491,000. Bureau of the Census, U.S. Dept. Of Commerce, Statistical Abstract of the United States 21 (1995). 288,133 over 32,672,000 yields .0088195 (or .88 percent). 288,133 over 15,491,000 yields .0186 (or 1.86 percent).

11. Robert M. Entman, *Journalism Quarterly*, Vol. 71, No. 3, Autumn 1994. And these scholarly findings find anecdotal support in my experience in the classroom: When I ask my students where they got their information about the L.A. riots that erupted after the first trial of the Simi Valley jury acquitted the officers who beat Rodney King, most point to the mass media. When I then ask for their sense of the demographics of those arrested for rioting, most students think the vast majority were Black. They are shocked to learn that about 60 percent of the arrests for "riot-related" violations were of Latinos ("Extra," *Focus on Racism in the Media*, July/Aug. 1992) and that 12 percent of those arrested for looting were White (Ishmael Reed, *Airing Dirty Laundry* 1993).

12. *See, e.g.*, Snyder, "On the Self-Perpetuating Nature of Social Stereotypes," in *Cognitive Processes in Stereotyping and Intergroup Behavior* 187-90 (D. Hamilton ed., 1981).

13. Patricia Williams, Notes From a Small World, *The New Yorker*, April 29 & May 6, 1996, at 90.

14. Sheri Lynn Johnson, "Race and the Decision to Detain a Suspect," 93 *Yale L.J.* 214, 238 (1983) (citing studies in Michael Argyle, *Bodily Communications* 73-105 (1975); Edward Twitchell Hall, *The Hidden Dimension* (1966); Edward Twitchell Hall, *The Silent Language* (1959); Paul Ekman, "Universal and Cultural Differences in Facial Expressions of Emotion," in *Nebraska Symposium on Motivation* (1971)).

15. "Developments in the Law—Race and the Criminal Process," 101 *Harv. L. Rev.* 1473, 1508 (1988) (footnotes omitted).

16. *Id.*

17. Guido Calabresi, *Ideals, Beliefs, Attitudes, and the Laws* 28 (1985).

18. *Chicago Tribune*, 11/30/94.

19. *U.S. News & World Report*, 1/17/94.

20. Norval Morris, "Race, Drugs and Imprisonment," *Chicago Tribune* Mar. 30, 1993, at 13.

21. Johnson, *supra* note 15, at 238.

22. Barbara D. Underwood, "Law and the Crystal Ball: Predicting Behavior with Statistical Inference and Individualized Judgment," 88 *Yale L.J.* 1408, 1422 n.40 (1979). Of course, as Professor Underwood notes, all predictions of human behavior pose some threat to the value of respect for individual autonomy. *Id.* But autonomy is especially threatened when the forecast that a person will choose to act violently is based on a factor—such as race—over which that person has no control. *Id.* at 1415-16, 1434-36.

23. Suzanna Sherry, "The Forgotten Victims," 63, *U. Colo. L. Rev.* 375, 375 (1992).

24. Pedestrian deaths alone accounted for more than 13 percent of traffic fatalities in the United States in 1994, according to the National Highway Traffic Safety Administration. Of 40,000 traffic-related deaths in 1994, nearly 5,500 were pedestrians, of which 800 were children age fifteen or under.

25. A study by the Texas Transportation Institute at Texas A&M University looked at highway deaths in the state four years before and

four years after rural speed limits were raised to 65 mph in 1987. The study found the serious accident rate rose 25 percent. (In 1993, an updated study showed the death and injury statistics went back to their levels before the speed limits increased in 1987.) According to the National Safety Council, a nongovernmental, not-for-profit public service organization dedicated to reducing accidental deaths and injuries, raising speed limits could jeopardize highway safety across the country.

26. Recall the discussion of reasonableness at the end of chapter 1, and see Judy Armour, "Race Ipsa Loquitur, Of Reasonable Racists, Intelligent Bayesians, and Involuntary Negrophobes," 46 *Stan. L. Rev.* 789-90 (1994).

27. *See generally* Sheri Lynn Johnson, "Black Innocence and the White Jury," 83 *Mich. L. Rev.* 1611, 1616-49 (1985); *see also* Douglas L. Colbert, "Challenging the Challenge: Thirteenth Amendment as a Prohibition against the Racial Use of Preemptory Challenges," 76 *Cornell L. Rev.* 1, 110-15 (1990).

28. See David C. Baldus, George Woodworth, & Charles A. Pulaski, Jr., "Comparative Review of Death Sentences: An Empirical Study of the Georgia Experience," 74 *J. Crim. L. & Criminology* 661 (1983); David C. Baldus, George Woodworth, & Charles A. Pulaski, Jr., *Equal Justice and the Death Penalty. A Legal and Empirical Analysis* (1990).

29. Johnson, *supra* note 28, at 1619-22, 1625-34 (revealing through social science research a historical tendency among Whites to be more lenient with White defendants than with Black ones).

30. Many American juries are all White or nearly all White both because of the racial composition of our population and because, for various reasons, the juror selection process results in underrepresentation of minorities. J. Van Dyke, *Jury Selection Procedures* 28-32, app. G (1977); Hayward R. Alker et al., "Jury Selection as a Biased Social Process," 11 *Law & Soc'y Rev.* 9, 33 (1976).

31. If juries were roughly half Black and half White, the biases of White and Black fact finders (both own-race and other-race) might tend to offset each other, reducing the influence of racial bias on the fact-finding process. But Blacks often have no voice in jury delibera-

tions, increasing the likelihood that the interests of Black victims will not be fully credited.

32. A restriction on the use of race-based statistics that might prejudice the jury in a self-defense case would be much like the Federal Rape Shield Law, *Fed. R. Evid.* 412, which prohibits the introduction of evidence of a victim's sexual history in a rape case. While prior sexual conduct is at least marginally probative of a victim's consent—just as racial crime statistics may be probative of a defendant's state of mind—Congress decided in the Rape Shield Law that the slight disadvantage to the defendant of prohibiting the evidence was outweighed by intrinsic justice concerns (minimizing distorted outcomes), as well as by extrinsic social policies (protecting the privacy interests of victims and encouraging reporting). *Fed. R. Evid.* 412 advisory committee's note. The intrinsic justice protections and extrinsic social policies which would be advanced by restricting the use of race-based statistical evidence in self-defense cases are as important as those advanced by the restrictions of the Rape Shield Law.

### Notes to Chapter 3

1. Micaela di Leonardo, "White Lies Black Myths: Rape, Race, and the Black 'Underclass,'" *Village Voice*, Sept. 22, 1992, at 30. Professor di Leonardo points out that she is an academic specialist on race, class, and gender in America, and that before her rape, she had been a rape crisis counselor and had taught classes on rape at Yale. *Id.*

2. *See* Holly Maguigan, "Battered Women and Self-Defense: Myths and Misconceptions in Current Reform Proposals," 140 *U. Pa. L. Rev.* 379, 409-12 (1991) (noting that most jurisdictions use a reasonableness standard that includes consideration of the defendant's individual circumstances and subjective point of view).

3. Holly Maguigan, a leading expert on women's self-defense work, notes that in a significant percentage of cases—about 20 percent—the defendant kills her abusive spouse in a "nonconfrontational" situation, i.e., a situation in which the decedent did not pose an imminent threat of death or serious bodily injury to the defendant. Maguigan, *supra* note 2, at 397.

4. Jandrucko v. Colorcraft/Fuqua Corp., No. 163-20-6245 (Fla. Dep't of Lab. & Empl. Sec. Apr. 26, 1990).

5. Judge John G. Tomlinson, Jr., ordered Fuqua Industries, the insurance carrier for Ms. Jandrucko's employer, to provide temporary total disability benefits to Ms. Jandrucko. Fuqua appealed the award to the Florida First District Court of Appeals, which affirmed Judge Tomlinson's decision per curiam without opinion. Colorcraft Corp. v. Jandrucko, 576 So. 2d 1320 (Fla. Dist. Ct. App. 1991). Fuqua thereafter unsuccessfully petitioned for a writ of certiorari from the United States Supreme Court. Fuqua Indus. v. Jandrucko, 111 S. Ct. 2893 (1991). While this petition was pending, Fuqua filed an original action under 42 U.S.C. § 1983 in the federal district court for the Southern District of Florida in an effort to enjoin the award of benefits. The Southern District denied Fuqua's request for preliminary relief, Fuqua Indus. v. Jandrucko, No. 91-842-CIV-KLR (S.D. Fla. 1991), and Fuqua appealed that decision. Prior to argument of that appeal, the district court dismissed Fuqua's complaint. Fuqua Indus. v. Jandrucko. No. 91-842-CIV-KLR (S.D. Fla. 1991). Fuqua also appealed that dismissal. The United States Court of Appeals for the Eleventh Circuit consolidated the two appeals for oral argument. At this stage of the proceedings, the American Civil Liberties Union filed an amicus curiae brief in support of Fuqua's appeal, and the NAACP provided counsel for Fuqua. On December 28, 1992, the Eleventh Circuit dismissed Fuqua's appeal without opinion. Fuqua Indus. v. Tomlinson, 983 F.2d 236 (11th Cir. 1992).

On March 2, 1993, the Florida Senate unanimously passed a bill that excludes from the definition of "accident" "any disease that manifests itself in the fear or dislike of an individual due to race, color, religion, sex, national origin, age, handicap, or marital status." 1993 Fla. Sess. Law Serv. 2352 (West).

6. *Jandrucko*, No. 163-20-6245, at 3. Ms. Jandrucko "testified [that] she was either punched or kicked in the back and knocked to the ground by a Black man who grabbed her purse and ran." Angela K. Calise, "WC Claim Cites Phobia of Black Men," *Nat'l Underwriter*, Sept. 9, 1991, at 3.

7. *Jandrucko*, No. 163-20-6245, at 4-5. One doctor testified that Ms. Jandrucko suffered from a posttraumatic stress disorder toward

Blacks, that she had an irrational fear of Black men, and that she experienced insomnia and horrifying nightmares due to the trauma of the mugging. The doctor recommended that she confront the phobic stimulus via progressive desensitization, biofeedback, and, perhaps, medication. He also testified that he felt Ms. Jandrucko to be honest and not at all deceitful or malingering, and that she was not predisposed to be fearful of or prejudiced toward Black persons. Another specialist testified that he had treated Ms. Jandrucko for what he diagnosed as a posttraumatic stress disorder. He also testified that even when Ms. Jandrucko rationally understood that she need not fear a particular situation, she still felt fear and demonstrated physiological signs of fear. He also said that she had become "hyper-vigilant" and became startled with even a minor stimulus. *Id.*

8. Testimony of Ruth Jandrucko at 26, Jandrucko, No. 163-20-6245 (Fla. Dep't Lab. & Employ. Sec. Apr. 4, 1986).

9. *Jandrucko*, No. 163-20-6245, at 6-7. A rehabilitation counselor testified that the relevant labor market offered no jobs in which Ms. Jandrucko would be guaranteed not to come into contact with African Americans. *Id.*

10. *Id.* at 10.

11. *Id.* at 8. Ms. Jandrucko testified that she was raised in a deeply religious Mennonite family which forbade prejudice toward others and viewed hard work as inherently good. *Id.* at 6. Her supervisor stated that Ms. Jandrucko was well liked by her colleagues, was not prejudiced against any ethnic groups, and was quite friendly with many of her Black coworkers prior to her accident. *Id.* at 3.

12. William Booth, "Phobia about Blacks Brings Workers' Compensation Award," *Wash. Post*, Aug. 13, 1992, at A3.

13. *Id.*

14. According to one leading proponent of the noninstrumental conception of legal liability: "The distinctive characteristic of non-instrumentalist claims is that their validity does not depend on the consequences of the court's decision. Whether a court protects judicial integrity or achieves a fair result turns on an assessment of the facts of the dispute, not on a correct prediction of what may follow." George P.

Fletcher, "Fairness and Utility in Tort Theory," 85 *Harv. L. Rev.* 537, 539 n.4 (1972).

15. George P. Fletcher, "The Individualization of Excusing Conditions," 47 *S. Cal. L. Rev.* 1269, 1270, 1293-95 (1974).

16. *Id.* at 1271.

17. For a detailed discussion of this point, see the discussion of the "Intelligent Bayesian" in chapter 3, specifically the section on the balance jurors must strike between the costs of waiting and the costs of not waiting.

18. *See* Robert S. Summers, "Pragmatic Instrumentalism in Twentieth-Century American Legal Thought—A Synthesis and Critique of Our Dominant General Theory about Law and Its Use," 66 *Cornell L. Rev.* 861 (1981).

19. Melvin A. Eisenberg, *The Nature of the Common Law* 8-9 (1988).

20. *Id.*

21. *See, e.g., Cal. Penal Code* § 26 (West 1988) (recognizing infancy and mental deficiency as culpability exceptions); *Tex. Penal Code Ann.* §§ 8.01-8.07 (West 1974 & Supp. 1994) (listing, *inter alia*, insanity and age as affecting criminal responsibility); *see also* Michael Andrew Tesner, "Racial Paranoia as a Defense to Crimes of Violence: An Emerging Theory of Defense or Insanity?" *11 B.C. Third World L.J.* 307, 333 (1991) (advocating treating racial-paranoia-induced delusional disorder as an insanity defense rather than a self-defense excuse).

22. Clarence E. Tygart, "Public Acceptance/Rejection of Insanity—Mental Illness Legal Defenses for Defendants in Criminal Homicide Cases," 20 *J. Psychiatry & Law* 375, 383 (1992).

23. John Hagan & Celesta Albonetti, "Race, Class, and the Perception of Criminal Injustice in America," 88 *Am. J. Soc.* 329 (1982) (presenting national survey data showing that Blacks are considerably more likely than Whites to perceive injustice in the judicial system).

## Notes to Chapter 4

1. *U.S. Const.* amend. XIV, § 1.

2. *E.g.,* Loving v. Virginia, 388 U.S. 1 (1967) (invalidating a state

prohibition of interracial marriage); Buchanan v. Warley, 245 U.S. 60 (1917) (striking down a Kentucky law forbidding Blacks to purchase homes in White neighborhoods); Strauder v. West Virginia, 100 U.S. 303 (1880) (invalidating a state restriction on jury service by Black citizens).

3. Korematsu v. United States, 323 U.S. 214 (1944); *see also* Laurence H. Tribe, *American Constitutional Law*, at 1465-74 (2d ed. 1988).

4. Dunn v. Blumenstein, 405 U.S. 330, 342 (1972); Shapiro v. Thompson, 394 U.S. 618, 634 (1968). Although the Supreme Court maintains that racial classifications are not per se invalid, racial classifications have so seldom survived judicial scrutiny that one leading commentator has referred to the strict scrutiny test as "'strict' in theory and fatal in fact." Gerald Gunther, "The Supreme Court 1971 Term—Foreword: In Search of Evolving Doctrine on a Changing Court: A Model for a Newer Equal Protection," 86 *Harv. L. Rev.* 1, 8 (1972).

5. 466 U.S. 429 (1984).

6. *Id.* at 433.

7. *Id.* at 434 (emphasis added). This language militates against narrowly reading *Palmore* to hold merely that a court may not consider racial factors when the only evidence of harm is speculation over potential social stigma. It suggests that the Court would have rejected even actual injury to the child as sufficient justification for caving in to popular prejudices and awarding custody to the father.

8. *Id.* at 433 (emphasis added).

9. Constitutional protections such as those offered by the Equal Protection Clause cannot be triggered in the absence of state action. I maintain that the courts' decisions to countenance the race-based evidence and legal arguments offered by the Reasonable Racist, the Intelligent Bayesian, and the Involuntary Negrophobe constitute the necessary state action. In the landmark civil rights case *Shelley v. Kraemer*, the Supreme Court held that judicial enforcement of racially restrictive covenants constitutes state action. In so holding, the Court acknowledged that state action may be found through the operation of the courts. For a fuller discussion, see Jody D. Armour, "Race Ipsa

Loquitur: Of Reasonable Racists, Intelligent Bayesians, and Involuntary Negrophobes," 46 *Stan. L. Rev.* 781, 807-08 (1994).

10. *Id.* at 808-09.

11. *See, e.g.,* Snyder, "On the Self-Perpetuating Nature of Social Stereotypes," in *Cognitive Processes in Stereotyping and Intergroup Behavior* 187-90 (D. Hamilton ed., 1981).

12. Micaela di Leonardo, "White Lies Black Myths: Rape, Race, and the Black 'Underclass,'" *Village Voice*, Sept. 22, 1992, at 30.

13. However, after moving to Northern California to stay with a friend weeks after the rape, di Leonardo "experienced . . . an uncomfortable but salutary shift: I was afraid of all the strange men I encountered[,] . . . nearly all [of whom] were white." *Id.*

14. Lon L. Fuller & Melvin Aron Eisenberg, *Basic Contract Law* 700 (5th ed. 1990).

15. *Id.*

16. "Tacit understandings" comprise culturally embedded ideals, beliefs, and attitudes about the world. According to theorists of cognitive psychology, many of an individual's beliefs and preferences develop through such understandings rather than explicit lessons. Because tacit understandings are not expressly stated, an individual learns and internalizes them without evaluating them at a conscious level. Although national news anchors like Dan Rather and Tom Brokaw do not announce that Blacks are "prone to violence" on the nightly news, the relentless (and arguably selective) representation of Black violence in the mass media tacitly transmits the same message. Even though most parents do not explicitly teach their children that Blacks are dangerous, the way a child's mother (perhaps unwittingly) clutches her purse and quickens her step when Blacks approach powerfully conveys the same lesson. *See* Charles R. Lawrence III, "The Id, the Ego, and Equal Protection: Reckoning with Unconscious Racism," 39 *Stan. L. Rev.* 317, 323, 336-39 (1987).

17. *Id.* at 338. Lawrence notes that [i]f an individual is hostile toward a group of people, she has an emotional investment in preserving the differentiations between her own group and the 'others[,]'" making the "preservation of inaccurate judgments about the outgroup . . . self-rewarding." *Id.* at 337.

18. Once an individual unconsciously internalizes a tacitly transmitted cultural stereotype, she unconsciously interprets experiences to be consistent with the underlying stereotype, selectively assimilating facts that validate the stereotype while disregarding those that do not. As a result, she views her negative attitudes toward Blacks as rational reflections of the observable world, rather than as culturally determined and constructed entities. *Id.* at 339; *see also* Snyder, *supra* note 11, at 183, 187-93.

19. Lawrence, *supra* note 16, at 349-55.

20. *Id.* at 351 (emphasis added). A lack of social respect denies Blacks "access to societal opportunities" and limits their "participat[ion] in society's benefits and responsibilities." *Id.* Moreover, "separate incidents of racial stigmatization do not inflict isolated injuries but are part of a mutually reinforcing and pervasive pattern of stigmatizing actions that cumulate to compose an injurious whole that is greater than the sum of its parts." *Id.; see also* Richard Delgado, "Words That Wound: A Tort Action for Racial Insults, Epithets, and Name-Calling," 17 *Harv. C.R.-C.L. L. Rev.* 133, 146 (1982); Kenneth L. Karst, "Foreword: Equal Citizenship Under the Fourteenth Amendment," 91 *Harv. L. Rev.* 1, 50-51 (1977).

21. Fuller & Eisenberg, *supra* note 14, at 702.

### Notes to Chapter 5

1. Following Elizabeth Schneider, a leading legal expert, I use the phrase "women's self-defense work" to denote "legal work on issues of sex-bias in the law of self-defense and criminal defenses generally." Elizabeth M. Schneider, "Describing and Changing: Women's Self-Defense Work and the Problem of Expert Testimony on Battering," 9 *Women's Rts. L. Rep.* 195, 197 at n.9 (1986). As Professor Schneider goes on to note, "The question of the admissibility of expert testimony on battered woman syndrome has been the primary legal issue which appellate courts have addressed in the area of women's self-defense work." *Id.* at 200.

2. For example, in the landmark self-defense case of *State v. Wanrow,* the trial judge—administering a pro-prosecution jury instruction

containing a narrow time restriction—directed the jury to evaluate the reasonableness of the defendant's fear of the decedent only in light of circumstances occurring "at or immediately before the killing." 559 P.2d 548, 555 (1977). The Supreme Court of the state of Washington held that the trial judge erred in limiting the time frame in this way, stating that "self-defense is to be evaluated in light of *all* the facts and circumstances known to the defendant, including those known substantially before the killing." *Id.* (emphasis in original).

3. An example of a social condition that prosecutors would prefer fact finders not to hear about in self-defense cases involving battered women is the lack of adequate protection from courts and police for battered women. As Schneider and Jordan note, "Women are forced to defend themselves against abuse because they do not receive adequate protection from the courts or from the police." Elizabeth M. Schneider & Susan B. Jordan, *Representation of Women Who Defend Themselves in Response to Physical or Sexual Assault,* 4 Women's Rights Law Reporter 149, 151 (1978). Economically, moreover, "[M]any women are forced to remain with their husbands out of economic necessity." *Id.* at 152.

4. In *State v. Wanrow,* the defendant's counsel challenged the lower court's self-defense jury instruction on the ground that it did not fully include the woman's perspective. 559 P.2d 548, 558.

5. A battered woman who kills in a nonconfrontational situation may make two quite distinct claims of reasonableness. The first claim maintains that she should be *excused* for errors in judgment attributable to the psychological disorders induced by her plight. The second claim maintains that her conduct was rational, and hence *justified,* in view of the objective obstacles that she faced; that is, she was justified in killing her batterer in a nonconfrontational situation in the same way that a hostage would be justified in killing the armed guard who inadvertently drops off to sleep.

Elizabeth Schneider points out that expert testimony on battered woman syndrome may address both of these claims. Expert testimony about "learned helplessness" and the psychological disorders induced by the abusive relationship taps an excuse theory of self-defense. In contrast, expert testimony about the objective obstacles to leaving—including "separation assault" (the often lethal escalation in violence that many women suffer when trying to leave a battering spouse) and the police's and courts' failure to protect women from ongoing abuse—suggests that the defendant's responses were rational and perhaps justified. Some feminists have cautiously criticized the learned helplessness element of battered woman syndrome for its tendency to promote stereotypes of women as passive, submissive, helpless, and irrational. Elizabeth M. Schneider, "Equal Rights to Trial for Women: Sex Bias in the Law of Self-Defense," 15 *Harv. C.R.-C.L. L. Rev.* 623 (1980).

6. *See, e.g.,* Mark Kelman, "Interpretive Construction in the Substantive Criminal Law," 33 *Stan. L. Rev.* 591, 643 (1981) (citing Glanville Williams, *Criminal Law: The General Part* [2d ed. 1961]) ("Ordinarily, we judge criminal liability at the moment the crime occurs. . . . The origin of a decision to act criminally is ordinarily of no concern").

7. See Schneider & Jordan, *Women's Self-Defense, supra* note 4, at 152 (noting that "[the] high and deadly incidence of wife-assault must be viewed with an understanding that many women are forced to remain with their husbands out of economic necessity or fear of retaliation. These problems are compounded by the shamefully few resources available to shelter battered women"); *see also* Martha R. Mahoney, "Legal Images of Battered Women: Redefining the Issue of Separation," 90 *Mich. L. Rev.* 1 (1991) (analyzing the phenomenon of lethal separation assault and the social circumstances in which it arises).

8. George Fletcher, *Rethinking Criminal Law* 799-800 (1978).

9. 28 N.E. 266 (Mass. 1891).

10. Peter Quinn sums up the prejudices confronted by Irish immigrants like Ms. O'Brien as follows:

Today the sense of the Catholic Irish as wholly alien to White, Christian society seems, perhaps, difficult to credit. But in mid-19th-century America the inalterable otherness of the Irish was for many a given. . . . Although eugenics was still a generation away, the theory of Irish racial inferiority was already being discussed. In 1860, Charles Kingsley, English clergyman and professor of modern history at Cambridge University, described the peasants he saw during his travels in Ireland in Darwinian terms: "I am daunted by the human chimpanzees I saw along that hundred miles of horrible country . . . to see White chimpanzees is dreadful; if they were Black, one would not feel it so much, but their skins, except where tanned by exposure, are as White as ours."

Three years later, in 1863, Charles Loring Brace, the founder of the Children's Aid Society and a prominent figure in the American social reform movement, published a book entitled *Races of the Old World.* Drawing on the claims of Anglo-Saxon racial superiority found in popular historical works such as Sharon Turner's *History of the Anglo-Saxon* and John Kemble's *The Saxon in England,* Brace located the cause of Irish mental deficiency in brain size, a measurement that served for Victorian ethnologists as an iron indication of intelligence: "The Negro skull, though less than the European, is within one inch as large as the Persian and the Armenian . . . . The difference between the average English and Irish skull is nine cubic inches, and only four between the average African and Irish."

Peter A. Quinn, "Closets Full of Bones: Racism and Anti-Immigration," *America,* Feb. 18, 1995, at 10.

11. Richard Delgado, "Ascription of Criminal States of Mind: Toward a Defense Theory for the Coercively Persuaded ('Brainwashed') Defendant," 63 *Minn. L. Rev.* 1, 11 (1978).

12. Joshua Dressler, "Professor Delgado's 'Brainwashing' Defense: Courting a Determinist Legal System," 63 *Minn. L. Rev.* 335, 342-43.

13. At least insofar as the evidence supported an *excuse* rather than a *justification* approach to the defendant's claim of self-defense. *See supra* note 6.

14. LaFave & Scott note that "there is a minority view, expressed in an occasional case and in a few manslaughter statutes, to the effect that the passion must be so great as to destroy the intent to kill, in order to accomplish the reduction of the homicide to voluntary manslaughter." LaFave & Scott, *Criminal Law* 572-73 (1972).

15. *Id.* at 572.

16. In discussing the provocation doctrine as it existed at common law, the Model Penal Code Commentaries to Section 210.3 state that "[p]rovocation is thus properly regarded as a recognition by the law that inquiry into the reasons for the actor's formulation of an intent to kill will sometimes reveal factors that should have significance in grading."

17. "The distinguishing feature of excusing conditions is that they preclude an inference from the act to the actor's character." Fletcher, *supra* note 9, at 799; "At most provocation affects the quality of the actor's state of mind as an indication of moral blameworthiness. . . . [Provocation doctrine] is a concession to human weakness and perhaps to non-deterability, a recognition of the fact that one who kills in response to certain provoking events should be regarded as demonstrating a significantly different character deficiency than one who kills in their absence." The *Model Penal Code Commentaries to Section 210.3*.

18. Mark Kelman, "Reasonable Evidence of Reasonableness," 17 *Critical Inquiry* 798, 802 (1991).

19. Martin Wasik, "Duress and Criminal Responsibility," 1977 *Crim. L. Rev.* 453, 453; *see also* State v. Woods, 357 N.E.2d 1059, 1066 (Ohio 1976) ("The essential characteristic of coercion . . . is that force, threat of force, strong persuasion or domination by another, necessitous circumstances, or some combination of those, has overcome the mind or volition of the defendant so that he acted other than he ordinarily would have acted in the absence of those influences"), *vacated in part*, 438 U.S. 910 (1978), *and overruled on other grounds by* State v. Downs, 364 N.E.2d 1140 (1977), *vacated in part*, 438 U.S. 909 (1978).

20. *See, e.g., D'Aquino v. United States*, 192 F.2d 338 (9th Cir. 1951), *cert. denied*, 343 U.S. 935 (1952); *Nall v. Commonwealth*, 208 Ky. 700 (1925).

21. *See, e.g., People v. Richards*, 269 Cal. App. 2d 768, 75 Cal. Rptr. 597 (1st Dist. 1969) (defendant cannot invoke defense of duress when parties threatening prisoner's life did not ask him to escape).

22. Commentary to Section 2.09 of the Model Penal Code.

23. *Id.*

24. *See, e.g.,* Fletcher, *supra* note 9, at 801 ("It goes without saying that a person's life experience may shape his character. Yet if we

excuse on the ground of prolonged social deprivation, the theory of excuses would begin to absorb the entire criminal law. . . . Now it may be the case that all human conduct is compelled by circumstances; but if it is, we should have to abandon the whole process of blame and punishment").

25. United States v. Brawner, 471 F.2d 969, 1032 (D.C. Cir. 1972) (Bazelon, C.J., concurring in part and dissenting in part).

26. David L. Bazelon, "The Morality of the Criminal Law," 49 *S. Cal. L. Rev.* 385 (1976). *Compare with* Richard Delgado, "'Rotten Social Background': Should the Criminal Law Recognize a Defense of Severe Environmental Deprivation?," 3 *Law & Ineq. J.* 9 (1985) (going beyond his earlier limited proposal of a "brainwashing" excuse to articulate a theory supporting a disadvantaged background excuse).

27. Bazelon, *supra* note 27, at 385, 395-96 (quoting United States v. Brawner, 471 F.2d 969, 1032 (D.C. Cir. 1972) (Bazelon, C.J., concurring in part and dissenting in part)).

28. *Id.* at 398.

29. Bob Herbert, "See-No-Evil Mayors," *N.Y. Times*, Jan. 8, 1996, at A-11.

30. *See* Fletcher, *supra* note 9, § 10.3.

31. *Id.* at 800-01 ("The distinguishing feature of excusing conditions is that they preclude an inference from the act to the actor's character. . . . Typically, if a bank teller opens a safe and turns money over to a stranger, we can infer that he is dishonest. But if he does all this at gunpoint, we cannot infer anything one way or the other about his honesty. . . . The same breakdown in the reasoning from conduct to character occurs in cases of insanity, for it is implicit in the medical conception of insanity that the actor's *true character* is distorted by his mental illness") (emphasis added).

32. "Provocation is said to be 'adequate' if it would cause a reasonable person to lose his self-control. *Of course, a reasonable person does not kill even when provoked,* but events may so move a person to violence that a homicidal reaction, albeit unreasonable in some sense, merits neither the extreme condemnation nor the extreme sanctions of a conviction of murder. The underlying judgment is thus that some instances of intentional homicide may be as much attributable to the

extraordinary nature of the situation as to the moral depravity of the actor." The *Model Penal Code Commentaries* to Section 210.3 (emphasis added).

33. See G. Fletcher, *supra* note 9, at 248; Wechsler & Michael, "A Rationale of the Law of Homicide II," 37 *Calum. L. Rev.* 1261, 1281-82 (1937) ("While it is true, it is also beside the point, that most men do not kill on even the gravest provocation; the point is that the more strongly they would be moved to kill . . . the less does [the actor's] succumbing serve to differentiate his character from theirs").

34. Fletcher, *supra* note 9, at 802 ("The circumstances surrounding the deed can yield an excuse only so far as they distort the actor's capacity for choice in a limited situation. The moral circumstances of an actor's life may account for some of his dispositions, but explaining a life of crime *cannot excuse particular acts* unless we wish to give up the entire institution of blame and punishment") (emphasis added).

35. Fletcher, *supra* note 9, at 801-02.

36. Fletcher, *supra* note 9, § 10.3.1.

37. Kelman, *supra* note 7, at 591, 647.

38. *N.Y. Times*, Feb. 1, 1996, at A8.

39. *N.Y. Times*, Feb. 1, 1996, at A8.

40. Moore remarks that our sympathy for the disadvantaged defendant "betokens a sense about one's self—as the seat of subjective will and responsibility—that one refuses to acknowledge in others." Michael S. Moore, "Causation and the Excuses," 73 *Calif. L. Rev.* 1091, 1147 (1985).

41. Sanford H. Kadish, "Excusing Crime," 75 *Calif. L. Rev.* 257, 280 (1987).

42. Id.

43. Kelman, *supra* note 7, at 591 n.144.

44. Nathan Caplan & Stephen D. Nelson, "On Being Useful: The Nature and Consequences of Psychological Research on Social Problems," 28 *Am. Psychologist* 199, 210 (1973).

45. Martin Kilson, "Anatomy of Black Conservatism," *Transition*, Issue 59, 11-12 (1993).

46. As relative newcomers to certain job markets from which they were undemocratically excluded, Blacks, Hispanics, and women are

not in the same position as White men to give preferential assistance to members of their own group.

47. *Wall Street Journal*, Apr. 2, 1985.

48. Id.

49. Guido Calabresi, *Ideals, Beliefs, Attitudes, and the Law* 1-19 (1985).

50. Norval Morris, "Race, Drugs and Imprisonment," *Chicago Trib.*, Mar. 30, 1993 at 13.

51. Id.

### Notes to Chapter 6

1. Cavagnuolo v. Baker & McKenzie, N.Y., State Div. Human Rights, No. 1B-E-D-86-115824, Dec. 17, 1993.

2. 273 N.E.2d 748 (Ill. App. Ct. 1971).

3. *Id.* (emphasis added).

4. James Henderson et al., *The Torts Process* (1994). Since the political slant of casebooks can have a lasting impact on the thinking of students and practitioners, I shall develop this point further. I teach torts to first-year students from *The Torts Process*, a popular problem-oriented casebook. The cases and materials in the book are organized around fabricated fact-patterns that afford students the opportunity to act out the roles of attorneys. One especially provocative problem involves a storekeeper who claims the privilege of self-defense after shooting a Black customer who the storekeeper mistakes for a robber. The storekeeper's privilege turns on whether a reasonable person would have believed he was under attack and the circumstances of the hypothetical shooting are sufficiently ambiguous to provide both sides of the dispute with plausible arguments. I assign students to represent both sides of the dispute and have them present their arguments as closing arguments to a mock jury.

Since studies show that most Americans consider race in assessing the risk of violence a person poses, *see, e.g.*, Tom W. Smith, *Ethnic Images* 4, 9-10, 16 (General Social Survey Topical Report No. 19, 1990) (on file with the author), the role that the Black victim's racial identity played in the storekeeper's decision to shoot cries out for recognition. Yet the students assigned to represent the Black victim's interest almost always eschew mentioning the racial factor. When I ask why they did not address the issue of the victim's racial identity, they invariably point to suggestions by the authors of the casebook that mentioning the racial factor would both violate the law and constitute a breach of professional responsibility.

5. Patricia Cohen, "WTC Lawyer Cites Bias against Arabs," *Newsday*, Feb. 19, 1994, at 18.

6. Todd J. Gillman, "Cook Jury Begins Deliberations, Claims Deadlock After Five Hours," *The Dallas Morning News*, Feb. 18, 1994, at 32A.

7. For example, in an often-quoted passage from his seminal article, "The Id, the Ego, and Equal Protection: Reckoning with Unconscious Racism," Professor Charles Lawrence III states:

> Americans share a common historical and cultural heritage in which racism has played and still plays a dominant role. Because of this shared experience, we also inevitably share many ideas, attitudes, and beliefs that attach significance to an individual's race and induce negative feelings and opinions about non-Whites. *To the extent that this cultural belief system has influenced all of us, we are all racists.*

Charles R. Lawrence III, "The Id, the Ego, and Equal Protection: Reckoning with Unconscious Racism," 39 *Stan. L. Rev.* 317, 322 (1987) (emphasis added).

8. Charles E. Case & Andrew M. Greeley, "Attitudes toward Racial Equality," 16 *Humboldt J. Soc. Rel.* 67, 68 (1990).

9. Charlotte Steeh & Howard Schuman, "Young White Adults: Did Racial Attitudes Change in the 1980s?" 98 *Am. J. Soc.* 340, 361 (1992).

10. Sheri Lynn Johnson, "Black Innocence and the White Jury," 83 *Mich. L. Rev.* 1611, 1648-49 (1985).

11. *Id.* at 1648.

12. *Id.* at 1650.

13. Harold Sigall & Richard Page, "Current Stereotypes: A Little Fading, a Little Faking," 18 *J. Personality & Soc. Psychol.* 247, 248 (1971).

14. *Id.* at 252. The subjects attributed the negative traits of ostentatiousness, laziness, ignorance, physical dirtiness, stupidity, and unreliability *more* often to Blacks when they thought the experimenter could monitor their uncontrolled physiological responses. Furthermore, they attributed the positive traits of intelligence, honesty, and sensitivity to Blacks *less* often in the pipeline condition. *Id.*

15. Johnson, *supra* note 10, at 1649-50. Johnson's interpretation of the meaning of these automatic responses reflects the interpretation given to them by the experimenters who designed the study, Harold Sigall and Richard Page. In their words, "[I]t will be obvious by this point that we have elected to interpret the results of the [bogus pipeline] condition as relatively distortion free, as more honest, and as "truer" than rating-condition responses. Thus, the [bogus pipeline] may be viewed as a lie detection device which facilitates truthful reporting." Sigall & Page, *supra* note 13, at 254.

16. Patricia G. Devine, "Stereotypes and Prejudice: Their Automatic and Controlled Components," 56 *J. Personality & Soc. Psychol.* 5, 6 (1989).

17. Phyllis A. Katz, "The Acquisition of Racial Attitudes in Children," in *Towards the Elimination of Racism* 125, 147 (Phyllis A. Katz ed., 1976).

18. Mary Ellen Goodman found that children at ages three to four already possess racial awareness, and 25 percent of four-year-olds expressed strong racial attitudes. Mary Ellen Goodman, *Race Awareness in Young Children* 47, 245, 252-54 (rev. ed. 1964). More recent research confirms that children typically show evidence of racial awareness by age three or four, and that by the time they reach first grade racial awareness is very well established. *See* Katz, *supra* note 17, at 125-26. Harold M. Proshansky, "The Development of Intergroup Attitudes," in 2 *Review of Child Development Research* 311, 314-15 (Lois Wladis Hoffman & Martin L. Hoffman eds., 1966). My personal experience with my own son locates the age of racial awareness even earlier. When my son was two years old, having just crossed the threshold of intelligible speech, he announced to his mother and me that his own (in my view, gloriously kinky) hair was "not pretty." Then, pointing to our television

and the image there of a model sporting cascading waves of decidedly unkinky hair for a shampoo commercial, he said, "Her hair pretty . . . mine not pretty."

19. Of course, a person can be prejudiced in favor of a group as well as against one. *See* Gordon W. Allport, *The Nature of Prejudice* 6-7 (1954). Since the focus of this book is the reactions of legal decision makers to outgroups, my focus is on prejudice against a group.

20. Anthony R. Pratkanis, "The Cognitive Representation of Attitudes," in *Attitude Structure and Function* 71, 91 (Anthony R. Pratkanis et al. eds., 1989).

21. Margo J. Monteith et al., "Prejudice and Prejudice Reduction: Classic Challenges, Contemporary Approaches," in *Social Cognition: Impact on Social Psychology* 323, 333-34 (Patricia G. Devine et al. eds., 1994).

22. Devine, *supra* note 16, at 5.

23. *See, e.g.*, Patricia G. Devine et al., "Prejudice with and without Compunction," 60 *J. Personality & Soc. Psychol.* 817, 817-19 (1991).

24. *See, e.g.*, id.

25. Devine et al., *supra* note 23, at 817.

26. Quoted in Daniel Coleman, "'Useful' Modes of Thinking Contribute to the Power of Prejudice," *N.Y. Times*, May 12, 1987, at C1, C10. Gordon Allport, another leading authority on stereotypes and prejudice, also has noted the conflict between ingrained stereotypes and new nonprejudiced beliefs. See Allport, *supra* note 19, at 328 ("Defeated intellectually, prejudice lingers emotionally").

27. The subjects' prejudice level was determined on the basis of their responses to a seven-item Modern Racism Scale, a nonreactive measure of negative attitudes toward Blacks. Devine et al., *supra* note 23, at 819. The Modern Racism Scale has proven to be useful in predicting a variety of behaviors including voting patterns and reactions to busing." Devine, *supra* note 16, at 7.

28. Devine et al., *supra* note 23, at 819. Two of the remaining four situations also focused on feelings subjects could have in response to situations involving Black people. One situation involved feeling upset that a Black couple moved in next door. The other involved feeling uncomfortable that a job interviewer is Black. The final two situations

focused on stereotypic thoughts subjects might have in contact situations with Black people. One thought situation involved seeing three middle-aged Black men on a street corner in the afternoon and thinking "Why don't they get a job?" The other thought situation involved seeing a Black woman with several small children and thinking "How typical." *Id.*

29. *Id.* at 820.

30. *Id.* at 822.

31. *Id.* at 827.

32. Devine, *supra* note 16, at 12-13.

33. *Id.* at 14.

34. In Johnson, Black Innocence and the White Jury, *supra* note 10, for example, Johnson argues that the perceived faking of nonprejudiced responses revealed in the "bogus pipeline" experiment is "complemented by observations concerning the prevalence of two kinds of racism. *Dominative* racists express their bigoted beliefs openly . . . while *aversive* racists do not want to associate with Blacks but do not often express this feeling." Johnson, *supra* note 10, at 1649. She notes that social scientists now believe that "aversive manifestations of racism increasingly predominate in all parts of the country." *Id.* Taken together, the dominative racist, the pseudoliberal, and the aversive racist make up the taxonomy of racists that frames the discussion of prejudice among legal scholars. And, inasmuch as "we are all racists," presumably we all fit into one of these subcategories. Alternatively, since proponents of the proposition that "we are all racists" at least recognize their racism, perhaps another category must be added to the current taxonomy of racists, such as the "enlightened racist."

35. Samuel L. Gaertner & John F. Dovidio, "The Aversive Form of Racism," in *Prejudice, Discrimination, and Racism* 61, 84 (John F. Dovidio & Samuel L. Gaertner eds., 1986).

36. Lawrence, *supra* note 7, at 335.

37. Johnson, *supra* note 10, at 1649.

38. Lawrence, *supra* note 7, at 335.

39. Peggy C. Davis, "Law as Microaggression," 98 *Yale L.J.* 1559, 1565 (1989) (quoting Gaertner & Dovidio, *supra* note 35, at 85-86).

40. Gaertner & Dovidio, *supra* note 35, at 67 ("Given the high salience of race and racially symbolic issues on questionnaires designed to measure racial prejudice, as well as aversive racists' vigilance and sensitivity to these issues, effective questionnaire measures of aversive racism, in our opinion, would be difficult if not impossible to develop").

41. Gaertner & Dovidio, *supra* note 35, at 77. In fact, White rescuers helped Blacks *more* often than Whites (94 percent to 81 percent). *Id.*

42. *Id.* In addition, when the subjects believed a bystander could intervene, they also showed "lower levels of arousal with Black than with White victims," as measured by their heart rate escalation when the accident occurred to the victim. *Id.* at 78.

43. *E.g.*, Davis, *supra* note 39, at 1562 (describing the projection of forbidden prejudices as a psychological defense mechanism); Lawrence, *supra* note 7, at 331-36 (explaining racism's relationship to Freud's psychoanalytic concepts of the Ego and the Id).

44. *See id.*; Jerome S. Bruner, "Social Psychology and Perception," in *Readings in Social Psychology* (Eleanor E. Maccoby et al. eds., 3d ed. 1958).

45. E. Tory Higgins & Gillian King, "Accessibility of Social Constructs: Information-Processing Consequences of Individual and Contextual Variability," in *Personality, Cognition, and Social Interaction* 69, 71-72 (Nancy Cantor & John F. Kihlstrom eds., 1981).

46. Steven L. Neuberg, "Behavioral Implications of Information Presented Outside of Conscious Awareness: The Effect of Subliminal Presentation of Trait Information on Behavior in the Prisoner's Dilemma Game," in 6 *Social Cognition* 207, 208 (1988).

47. *Id.*

48. E. Tory Higgins et al., "Category Accessibility and Impression Formation," 13 *J. Experimental Soc. Psychol.* 141, 141-45 (1977).

49. *Id.* at 145-46. Some subjects were momentarily exposed to favorable trait terms (e.g., "adventurous"), some to unfavorable trait terms (e.g., "reckless"), and some to trait terms that were inapplicable to the behavior of the protagonist in the passage the subjects were about to read (e.g., "obedient" or "disrespectful"). *Id.* at 145.

50. *Id.* at 145. Specifically, the paragraph was ambiguous with respect to several personality traits. For example, the protagonist of the paragraph was described as thinking about crossing the Atlantic in a sailboat, behavior that could be characterized favorably as "adventurous" or unfavorably as "reckless." *Id.*

51. *Id.*

52. Birt L. Duncan, "Differential Social Perception and Attributes of Intergroup Violence: Testing the Lower Limits of Stereotyping of Blacks," 34 *J. Personality & Soc. Psychol.* 590, 595-97 (1976). Duncan had ninety-six White undergraduates individually rate a series of interactions between two "other subjects" that culminated in an ambiguous shoving event. The two "other subjects" (both male) were actually confederates acting out a script. The experimental session consisted of a videotape of the two actors discussing a hypothetical problem; however, the subject who observed the tape was led to believe that the discussion actually was taking place in another room. *Id.* at 592. The subject was asked to evaluate the behavior of the "actors" six times at precise intervals, which the experimenter signaled to him during the tape. *Id.* To evaluate the actors' behavior, the subjects had to fit the behavior into one of ten major categories on a rating form. The ten major categories were *dramatizes, gives information, gives opinion, gives suggestion, asks for information, asks for opinion, asks for suggestion, playing around, aggressive believer, and violent behavior. Id.* at 594. The subjects' final evaluations—their sixth ratings—were designed to coincide with the heated discussion and ambiguous shove near the end of the interactions; thus, this sixth rating was the major dependent measure. *Id.* at 592.

The major independent variables were the racial identities of the actor who initiated the ambiguous shove (the "protagonist") and the actor who received the shove (the "victim"). *Id.* The subjects were randomly assigned to one of the following experimental conditions (tapes): Black protagonist-White victim; White protagonist-Black victim; Black protagonist-Black victim; White protagonist-White victim. *Id.* at 592-94. The results of this experiment are disturbing and unequivocal. When the protagonist was Black and the victim White, 75 percent of the subjects characterized the ambiguous shove as "violent behavior," whereas when the protagonist was White and the victim Black, only 17 percent so characterized it. On the other hand, 42 percent of the subjects perceived the shove as "playing around" or "dramatizing" when the protagonist was White and the victim Black, compared with only 6 percent in the Black protagonist-White victim conditions. *Id.* at 595. The discrepancy between White protagonist-White victim condition and Black protagonist-Black victim condition is also drastic: 69 percent of the subjects perceived the within-group (Black-Black) condition as violent compared with 13 percent in the White-White conditions. *Id.* Thus, the subjects in this experiment were much more likely to characterize an act as violent when it was performed by a Black than when the same act was committed by a White. *Id.*

53. *Id.*

54. H. Andrew Sager & Janet Ward Schofield, "Racial and Behavioral Cues in Black and White Children's Perceptions of Ambiguously Aggressive Acts," 39 *J. Personality & Soc. Psychol.* 590, 594-97 (1980).

55. "The accessibility of a construct will increase when the estimate of the likelihood of occurrence of a construct instance increases." Higgins & King, *supra* note 46, at 75. For example, in Harold Kelley's study of labeling effects on impression formation, students' ratings of a new instructor were more favorable when the experimenter described the instructor as a "warm" person to the students before the instructor's arrival than when the experimenter described the instructor as a "cold" person. Harold H. Kelley, "The Warm-Cold Variable in First Impressions of Persons," 18 *J. Personality & Soc. Psychol.* 431, 435 (1950). According to Kelley, the experimenter's poor description prepared the students to expect instances of the category designated by the label as well as instances of other categories assumed to be closely related to this category (e.g., "friendly" and "helpful"). *Id.* at 435-36.

56. This is also another possible interpretation of the results of Kelly's study—that the mere exposure to the label "warm" may have activated the trait category designated by the label. Higgins & King, *supra* note 46, at 73-74. This passive priming effect would have con-

stituted what I shall refer to later in the article as an "automatic process." Furthermore, because both processes—the controlled and the automatic—could have simultaneously operated on the same underlying category ("warm" or "warm disposition"), the two processes were probably mutually facilitative, such that both served to make the underlying category more accessible. What happens, however, when the two processes are mutually antagonistic, i.e., when the controlled processes activate one category or knowledge structure while the automatic processes activate a very different category or knowledge structure? Which process determines which knowledge structure the perceiver will use to judge another person? I address these critical questions below.

57. David L. Ronis et al., "Attitudes, Decisions, and Habits as Determinants of Repeated Behavior," in *Attitude Structure and Function* 213, 218 (Anthony R. Pratkanis et al. eds., 1989).

58. *Id.*

59. 1 William James, *Principles of Psychology* 112 (1890) (quoting William B. Carpenter, *Principles of Mental Physiology* 339-345 [1874]).

60. *Id.* at 112-14. Thus, like the need to think in terms of simplifying categories, the mind's need to form habits arises from the fact that it is a limited capacity processor.

61. Walter Schneider & Richard M. Shiffrin, "Controlled and Automatic Human Information Processing: I. Detection, Search, and Attention," 84 *Psychol. Rev.* 1, 2-3 (1977).

62. Ronis et al., *supra* note 58, at 219.

63. Devine, *supra* note 16, at 6.

64. *Id.*

65. Ronis et al., *supra* note 58, at 220-22.

66. *Id.*

67. The content of a stereotype may be based partly on the unequal distribution of members of different groups in different social roles. Researchers have found that observing members of different groups in different roles can influence the actual content of stereotypes. *See* Alice H. Eagly & Valerie J. Steffen, "Gender Stereotypes Stem from the Distribution of Women and Men into Social Roles," 46 *J. Person-*

*ality & Soc. Psychol.* 735, 751-52 (1984). A prominent social psychologist who spent a year as a high school exchange student in the Republic of South Africa described how an observer in that country could learn negative Black stereotypes from the social environment:

> Groups of supervised Black prisoners were often seen in local parks and on municipal property performing gardening and maintenance tasks. White prisoners, on the other hand, were not required to perform these tasks in public. What might be the implication of seeing only Black prisoners fill these roles? First, one might conclude that Blacks are more likely to engage in criminal behavior than Whites. Whereas relatively few White prisoners were ever seen in public, Black convicts were regularly on display in the community. Second, one might conclude that Blacks are particularly adept at tasks such as gardening and maintenance, given that they are seen performing these tasks every day. Thus, the White South Africans' stereotype that Blacks are criminally prone and capable primarily of certain types of labor may arise from seeing them on a daily basis in these roles.

David Hamilton et al., "Social Cognition and the Study of Stereotyping," in *Social Cognition: Impact on Social Psychology* 291, 310 (Patricia G. Devine et al. eds., 1994).

68. Strong evidence of systematic and widespread manipulation of stereotypes in news reporting and other aspects of the mass media has been well documented by FAIR (Fairness & Accuracy In Reponing), a national media watch group, in "Focus on Racism in the Media," 5 *EXTRA!*, July/Aug. 1992.

69. Devine, *supra* note 16, at 6.

70. Ronis et al., *supra* note 58, at 232.

71. Devine, *supra* note 16, at 6.

72. *Id.* at 16.

73. *Id.* at 9-10. To prevent subjects from having conscious access to the labels, or "primes," Devine presented the primes to the subjects' parafoveal visual field (i.e., outside the fovea, the area of the most distinct vision on the retina). A separate test with different subjects had

determined that under these conditions subjects could not recall or recognize the primes. *Id.* at 8-10.

74. One set of primes included the following twelve words: nigger, poor, afro, jazz, slavery, musical, Harlem, busing, minority, oppressed, athletic, and prejudice. The other set of primes included the following: Negroes, lazy, Blacks, blues, rhythm, Africa, stereotype, ghetto, welfare, basketball, unemployed, and plantation. *Id.* at 10.

75. *Id.* at 11-12.

76. Research shows that the accessibility of a construct will also increase if the accessibility of a closely related category is increased. For example, studies in cognitive literature have shown that subjects recognize or process a word faster when the word (e.g., butter) is preceded by an associated word (bread) than an unassociated word (e.g., nurse). *See generally* David E. Meyer et al., "Loci of Contextual Effects on Visual Word Recognition," in *Attention and Performance* 98 (Patrick M. A. Rabbit & Stanislav Dornic eds., 1975). Research on social cognition has found the same priming effects for closely associated social constructs. For example, a 1955 study found that activating one social construct (reading about the life of Pope Pius XII) will increase the accessibility of closely related social constructs (the principles of the Catholic Church). Higgins & King, *supra* note 46, at 82-83. There is also evidence that constructs with a similar evaluative tone are closely related, so that activating a social construct (e.g., ugly) should also increase the accessibility of evaluatively similar social constructs (e.g., evil, gangster, mugging). *See* Delos D. Wickens, "Characteristics of Word Encoding," in *Coding Processes in Human Memory* 191 (Arthur W. Melton & Edwin Martin eds., 1972).

77. Although the dissociation model focuses on individual-level conflict between more egalitarian and less prejudiced beliefs on the one hand, and persistent prejudice-like responses on the other, I am not suggesting that high-prejudiced people no longer exist. Jennifer L. Hochschild and Monica Herk, for example, have pointed out that a small group of "hard-core" racists still exists in America. Jennifer L. Hochschild & Monica Herk, "'Yes, but . . .': Principles and Caveats in American Racial Attitudes," in *NOMOS XXXII: Majorities and Minorities* 308, 311 (John W. Chapman & Alan Wertheimer eds.,

1990). As recently as 1978, as many as 15 percent of White adults believed that "Blacks are inferior to White people." *Id.* (Moreover, with the publicity surrounding recently released books like *The Bell Curve*, which is essentially an apology for the subordination of Blacks in this country, the number of people who endorse derogatory Black stereotypes may be on the rise.) Reducing the bias of "hard-core" racists—people whose personal beliefs overlap derogatory Black stereotypes—poses special challenges for lawyers and judges concerned about reducing courtroom bias. Perhaps Rokeach's self-confrontation technique, *see infra* note 88, could be employed in some extreme cases. However, in light of social science data indicating that prejudice has been declining steadily over the past forty years, I am proceeding on the assumption that many (if not most) present-day jurors hold nonprejudiced personal beliefs that may be activated in the service of less-biased social judgments. Insofar as this assumption does not hold in a given case, other techniques (e.g., Rokeach's self-confrontation technique) may be called for.

78. For example, by using a semantic priming task in which the presentation of a word unconsciously influences subsequent processing of related words. James H. Neely has demonstrated that when automatic processing produced a response that conflicts with conscious expectation (induced through experimenter instructions, subjects inhibit the automatic response and intentionally replace it with one consistent with their conscious expectation. James H. Neely, "Semantic Priming and Retrieval from Lexical Memory: Roles of Inhibitionless Spreading Activation and Limited-Capacity Attention," 106 *J. Experimental Psychol.* 226, 251-53 (1977).

79. The salience of the subjects' gender was manipulated by varying the sexual composition of the different experimental groups. For example, in one series of experiments, a female experimenter conducted twenty groups of subjects each composed of two or three females and one male, and a male experimenter conducted twenty groups of subjects each composed of two or three males and one female. Higgins & King, *supra* note 46, at 86. The researchers reasoned that "gender should be more salient for a group member whose gender is in the minority than for a group member whose gender is in the majority." *Id.* at 85.

80. *Id.* at 87-88. In Study 1, the subjects (146 college students) in half of the groups read a paragraph supposedly describing a female undergraduate at Princeton (Barbara) and subjects in the other half of the groups read the same paragraph ambiguously describing a male undergraduate (Bob). *Id.* at 86-87. The paragraph was constructed to unambiguously exemplify the following eight traits: two evaluatively positive, stereotypically male traits (active, ambitious), and two evaluatively negative, stereotypically male traits (aggressive, selfish); two evaluatively positive, stereotypically female traits (polite, sensitive), and two evaluatively negative, stereotypically female traits (emotional, dependent). *Id.* at 86. After reading the paragraph, the subjects were given a twenty-minute filler task to take their minds off the paragraph they had just read. They were then asked to reproduce the paragraph about Bob (Barbara) as best they could, word for word. *Id.* at 87.

When the person described in the paragraph was ostensibly male (Bob), the subjects recalled less stereotypically male and more stereotypically female information about him when their gender was in the minority (i.e., high gender salience) than when their gender was in the majority (i.e., low gender salience). *Id.* Moreover, when the person described in the paragraph was ostensibly female (Barbara), the subjects recalled less stereotypically female information about her when their gender was in the minority than when it was in the majority. *Id.* Similar results were found in a different study in which subjects (fifty-eight college students) were again put into groups containing a solitary male or female and simply asked to "tell us about yourself" in writing. *Id.* at 103. "[M]ales in the minority described themselves as more stereotypically female and less stereotypically male than males in the majority, whereas females in the minority described themselves as more stereotypically male and less stereotypically female than females in the majority." *Id.* at 104. Thus, when the college students' gender was relatively salient, they were more likely to describe themselves in terms of nontraditional or modern views of male and female attributes. *Id.* Otherwise, their spontaneous self-descriptions (as well as their descriptions of others) tend to reflect the prevailing sexual stereotypes. *Id.*

81. *Id.* at 85-86.

82. *Id.* at 87-88, 104-05; *cf. supra* notes 32-33 and accompanying text (suggesting similar psychological processes involved in respondents' expressions of nonprejudiced thoughts about Blacks in an anonymous thought-listing task).

83. *See* Margo J. Monteith, "Self-Regulation of Prejudiced Responses," 65 *J. Personality & Soc. Psychol.* 469, 478-84 (1993) (describing an experiment in which low-prejudice subjects effectively inhibited prejudiced responses to jokes about gays when experimenters alerted them to discrepancies between their nonprejudiced personal standards and their discriminatory tendencies).

84. *Id.* at 234-35, 252, 257 (quoting Clarence Darrow's closing argument).

85. Recall Harold Kelley's study of labeling effects on impression formation discussed *supra* at note 56. In that study, students' ratings of a new instructor were more favorable when the experimenter described the instructor as a "warm" person to the students before the instructor's arrival than when the experimenter described the instructor as a "cold" person. Kelley's interpretations of these results was that the experimenter's poor description gave the students a conscious expectation for instances of the category designated by the label (e.g., "warm") as well as other categories such as "friendly" and "helpful" assumed to be closely related to that category. That is, the students' ratings were driven by controlled processes. Kelley, *supra* note 56, at 433-35. Higgins and King suggest that another possibility is that exposure to a particular label automatically activated the category designated by the label as well as other categories assumed to be closely related to that category. From this perspective, the students' ratings were driven by automatic processes. Higgins & King, *supra* note 46, at 73-74. In the end, Higgins and King suggest that the students' ratings were probably influenced by both controlled and automatic processes; in their words, Kelley's "findings are likely to have been multiply determined." *Id.* at 74. *See also* John A. Bargh et al., "The Additive Nature of Chronic and Temporary Sources of Construct Accessibility," 50 *J. Personality & Soc. Psychol.* 869, 870 (1986) (discussing how different accessibility influences operating within the same per-

son at the same time "may be mutually *facilitative*, such that both serve to make a single construct more accessible").

86. Darrow was employing a strategy for changing highly prejudiced attitudes similar to what fifty years later came to be known as the Rokeach's confrontation technique. *See* Milton Rokeach, *The Nature of Human Values* 286-306 (1973). Rokeach's strategy was inspired by Gunner Myrdal's characterization of the American Dilemma. 1 Gunner Myrdal, *An American Dilemma: The Negro Problem and Modern Democracy* 89, 1139-41 (1944). According to Myrdal, many White Americans, who are committed to the general egalitarian tenets of the "American Creed," but who simultaneously have specific prejudiced tendencies, experience an intimal moral conflict. Rokeach reasoned that self-dissatisfaction arises when people are encouraged to recognize the discrepancy between their egalitarian self-conception and their prejudiced responses. This self-dissatisfaction should then motivate individuals to change the prejudiced aspects of their responses to be more in line with their egalitarian self-image.

87. George P. Fletcher, *A Crime of Self-Defense: Bernhard Goetz and Law on Trial* 206 (1988). One such trial tactic involved re-creating the shooting of the teenagers, for which the defense called in four "props" to act as the four Black victims:

> The nominal purpose of the demonstration was to show the way in which each bullet entered the body of each victim. The defense's real purpose, however, was to re-create for the jury, as dramatically as possible, the scene that Goetz encountered when four young Black passengers began to surround him. For that reason [Goetz's attorney] asked the Guardian Angels to send him four young Black men to act as the props in the demonstration. In came the four young Black Guardian Angels, fit and muscular, dressed in T-shirts, to play the parts of the four victims in a courtroom minidrama.

*Id.* at 207. Although the witness whom these Black men surrounded was not authorized to testify about the typical person's fear of being accosted by four such individuals, the defense "designed the dramatic scene so that the implicit message of menace and fear would be so strong that testimony would not be needed." *Id.* at 130.

88. *Id.* at 206. As Fletcher insightfully notes:

> These verbal attacks signaled a perception of the four youths as representing something more than four individuals committing an act of aggression against a defendant. That "something more" requires extrapolation from their characteristics to the class of individuals for which they stand. There is no doubt that one of the characteristics that figures in this implicit extrapolation is their blackness.

*Id.*

89. "[A]ny word, metaphor, argument, comment, action, gesture, or intonation" that resonates with derogatory racial stereotype constitutes racial imagery. Sheri L. Johnson, "Racial Imagery in Criminal Cases," 67 *Tul. L. Rev.* 1739, 1799 (1993).

90. To this point, I have focused on the descriptive content of stereotypes. Recent research has also begun to investigate the *automatic affective* processing effects associated with racial category priming. Negative attitudes and emotional responses to Blacks—hatred, loathing, disgust, fear, etc.—have historically accompanied the negative personality traits associated with Blacks. Thus, priming the racial category probably also primes negative responses that are associated with the category. This proposition is consistent with Gordon Allport's observation that a category such as a racial group category "saturates all that it contains with the same ideational and emotional flavor." *Allport, supra* note 19, at 21.

91. *Fletcher, supra* note 89, at 208.

92. Patricia J. Williams, *The Alchemy of Race and Rights* 77 (1991).

93. Smith v. State, 516 N.E.2d 1055, 1064 (Ind. 1987), *cert. denied,* 488 U.S. 934 (1988).

94. People v. Lurry, 395 N.E.2d 1234, 1237 (Ill. App. Ct. 1979).

95. State v. Noel, 693 S.W.2d 317, 318 (Mo. Ct. App. 1985).

96. Commonwealth v. Graziano, 331 N.E.2d 808, 812 (Mass. 1975) (in a case involving recent immigrants, prosecutor's reference to Al Capone and "the godfather").

97. Soap v. Carter, 632 F.2d 872, 878 (10th Cir. 1980) (Seymour, J., dissenting), *cert. denied*, 451 U.S. 939 (1981) (in case involving American Indians, prosecutor's statement that "when you see an Indian that drinks liquor, you see a man that can't handle it" and that "they can't manage it").

98. *See* Johnson, *supra* note 91, at 1753-56.

99. *Id.* at 1760-62.

100. *See* Lawrence, *supra* note 7, at 355 (arguing that the prevalence of unconscious discrimination thwarts intent analysis). Lawrence argues for a "cultural meaning test," by which governmental conduct would be evaluated "to see if it conveys a symbolic message to which the culture attaches racial significance." *Id.* at 356. *See also* Elizabeth L. Earle, "Banishing the Thirteenth Juror: An Approach to the Identification of Prosecutorial Racism," 92 *Colum. L. Rev.* 1212, 1239-40 (1992) (arguing that adapted to prosecutorial forensics, Lawrence's cultural meaning test can become a reasonable person standard—i.e., whether a reasonable person would construe the reference to have a racial tenor—and that indirect references to race should be gauged according to this standard).

101. Johnson, *supra* note 91, at 1799-1800. Employing the term "racial imagery" to refer to any racial reference, whether blatant or subtle, Johnson proposes the following test for racial imagery:

"Racial imagery" is any word, metaphor, argument, comment, action, gesture, or intonation that suggests, either explicitly or through commonly understood allusion, that

(1) a person's race or ethnicity affects his or her standing as a full, capable, and decent human being; or

(2) a person's race or ethnicity in any way affects the credibility of that person's assertions; or

(3) a person's race or ethnicity in any way affects the likelihood that he or she would choose a particular course of conduct whether criminal or noncriminal; or

(4) a person's race or ethnicity in any way affects the appropriate sanctions for a crime committed by or against him or her; or

(5) a person's race or ethnicity sets him or her apart from

members of the jury, or makes him or her allied with members of the jury or, more generally, that a person's race or ethnicity allies him or her with other persons of the same race or ethnic group or separates him or her from persons of another race or ethnic group.

Racial imagery will be conclusively presumed from the unnecessary use of a racially descriptive word.

Where a metaphor or simile uses the words "white," "black," "brown," "yellow," or "red"; where any companions to animals of any kind are made; or where characters, real or fictional, who are strongly identified with a racial or ethnic group are referred to, racial imagery will be presumed, subject only to rebuttal through proof that the term in question could not have racial connotations with respect to any witness, defendant, attorney, or judge involved in the case.

That a speaker disclaims racial intent, either contemporaneously or at a later date, shall have no bearing upon the determination of whether his or her remarks or actions constitute a use of racial imagery.

*Id.*

102. A group reference should be chargeable to an attorney if he knows or reasonably should know that a witness will make such a reference and does not take reasonable steps (e.g., remonstration of the witness) to prevent the reference. Under the current code of professional conduct, an attorney is obligated not to offer false evidence, including putting a witness on the stand when she anticipates false testimony. *Model Rules of Professional Conduct*, Rule 3.3(a)(4) (1994). Our growing understanding of social cognition suggests that inappropriate and unchecked references to stereotyped groups (including their symbolic equivalent) subvert justice and accurate truth seeking as much as perjury. In fact, covert group references may subvert truth seeking even more than perjury to the extent that jurors discount the testimony of defendants, based on their commonsense understanding that such witnesses have substantial incentives to lie. But coven group references can distort jurors' social judgments unconsciously, thus

depriving them of the opportunity to weigh and discount the reference in the way they could the testimony of defendants.

103. An example of a proper reference to race would be one in which race is part of a description given for the purpose of identification.

104. In arguing that color-blind legal proceedings may impair the capacity of legal decision makers to inhibit habitual prejudice—like responses and activate newer nonprejudiced ones, I decidedly am not suggesting that legal proceedings should be open to any and all racial references, however invidious. To the contrary, in the first four chapters of this book, I argued unequivocally against the use of race-based claims of reasonableness in self-defense claims, even though race may be formally relevant to such claims. On a strictly formal level, therefore, it may seem that I am taking a paradoxical position on the appropriateness of racial references in legal proceedings: legal decision makers should and should not consider race in resolving legal disputes. The paradox dissolves, however, as soon as we scratch beneath the superficial layer of formalism and consider the distinction between racial references that subvert the rationality of the fact-finding process and racial references that enhance that rationality.

105. Andrew Hacker, *Two Nations* 32 (1992).

106. Stanton by Brooks v. Astra Pharmaceutical Products, Inc., 718 F.2d 553 (3d Cir. 1983). I am indebted to Professor Frank McClellan for bringing this case to my attention. Professor McClellan was co-counsel on this case. Both he and his partner are Black, and they frequently try cases before predominantly White juries on behalf of Black plaintiffs.

107. *Id.* at 578-79 (quoting from the trial transcript).

108. *Id.* (citing Draper v. Airco, Inc., 580 F.2d 91, 95 [3d Cir. 1978]). Notwithstanding this court's efforts to compel Professor McClellan and his partner to adopt a color-blind approach to trying cases for Black clients, Professor McClellan reports that he and his partner still frequently challenge jurors to be unbiased in judging the claims of their Black clients.

109. *See, e.g.,* Douglas L. Colbert, "Challenging the Challenge: Thirteenth Amendment as a Prohibition against the Racial Use of Preemptory Challenges," 76 *Cornell L. Rev.* 1, 110-115 (1990) (discussing empirical findings that all-White juries are not always impartial).

110. *See, e.g.*, Daniel Coleman, "Study Finds Jurors Often Hear Evidence with a Closed Mind," *N.Y. Times*, Nov. 29, 1994, at C1. Furthermore, being human, judges are no less subject to unconscious, prejudice-like responses than jurors. Thus, judges might also benefit if rationality-enhancing comments are made at opening statements.

# INDEX

affirmative action, 107–108, 155
American Civil Liberties Union,
   47
Amherst, 109
antideterminism, 89, 97, 101
apartheid, 56
*Armour v. Salisbury*, 10
arrest rates. *See* crime rates
assumed risk, 112
aversive racism model, 128–129

Bailey, Billy, 102
battered children, 96–97
battered women, 6–7, 26, 62, 67,
   81–83, 91, 112–113
battered women syndrome. *See* battered women
Bayes, Sir Thomas, 36
Bayesian, 35–36, 38–42, 43, 45–47,

49– 50, 57, 60, 62, 68, 71–72, 80,
   156
Bazelon, Judge David, 95–96, 103,
   106
Bell, Derrick, 13
Big Kahuna, 29
Bill of Rights, 32
*Birth of a Nation,* 144
Black Tax, 1, 13–17, 54, 118, 155
*Brown v. Board of Education,* 31
Bruner, Jerome S., 130

cab drivers, 45, 56, 57
Calabresi, Guido, 43, 111
Campriello, Austin, 118
Caplan, Nathan, 107
Cohen, Richard, 8, 35–36
Coleman, Anne, 102–103
color-blind perspective. *See* formalism

color-consciousness, 60
concentration camps, U.S., 32
consent, 85, 87
conservatives, 24, 29, 36, 99, 108
Copernicus, 24
crime rates, 8, 15–16, 37, 38, 39, 40,
    42–45, 51, 113, 147
cultural defense, 28–29
cultural differences, 42

Darrow, Clarence, 141–146,
    149–150, 153
*Daubert Case*, 24
*Death of Common Sense*, 24
Delgado, Richard, 90–91, 96
desegregation, 31
determinism, 89, 92–94, 96, 99, 101,
    110
*Detroit Free Press*, 141
Devine, Patricia, 121, 134, 136, 138
di Leonardo, Micaela, 61–62, 73, 76
discrimination: education, 12, 44;
    employment, 12, 44, 113, 154;
    mathematical, 7; racial, 8, 12, 13,
    15, 21, 34, 42, 56–58, 69, 73, 79,
    95, 127–128, 145, 156, 158;
    rational, 3, 8, 16, 35, 156, 158;
    reverse, 6, 108, 110; unconscious,
    14, 16, 73, 75, 77, 106, 118,
    129–130, 134, 137, 139, 143–144,
    151, 154–155, 158
dissociation model, 124, 148
Dressler, Joshua, 91
D'Souza, Dinesh, 8
Du Bois, W. E. B., 158
duress, 92–93

education. *See* discrimination, edu-
    cation
empirical studies, 17
Equal Protection Clause, Fourteenth
    Amendment, 69–71, 73, 77–78

Evil Deity, 111
externalists, 30

FBI Uniform Crime Reports, 40
*flagrante delicto*, 104
Fletcher, George, 96, 99–101, 145–146
formalism, 6–8, 115, 117–118, 151, 153
free speech, 30
Fuhrman, Mark, 14

Galileo, 24
gerrymandering, 105
Glasser, Ira, 47
God's-eye perspective, 30
Goetz, Bernhard 4, 145–146, 148
Graduate Record Exam, 155

Hand, Learned, 33
Harvard Law School, 44
Hernstein, Richard, 13
Howard, Philip, 24

instrumentalists, 64–65, 77–79
internalists, 30–31
interracial marriage. *See* miscegena-
    tion
Involuntary Negrophobe, 27, 61–62

*Jackson v. Chicago Transit Authority*,
    117
Jackson, Jesse, 16, 35, 43, 45
Jackson, Samuel L., 29
James, William, 134
Jandrucko, Ruth, 63–64, 72, 76
Jefferson, Thomas, 28–29
Jim Crow, 143
Johnson, Sheri Lynn, 119–120, 122,
    124
Judeo-Christian dogma, 30
juries, 6, 21, 26, 59, 60, 65, 72, 95,
    100, 115, 117, 119, 142–144,
    146–147, 149, 151–152

jurors. *See* juries

Katz, Phyllis, 121
Kelman, Mark, 105
King, Martin Luther, Jr., 118
King, Rodney, 5, 65–66
Koon, Stacey C., 5
Ku Klux Klan, 13, 144

legacies, 108–109
Leviathan state, 17
Levin, Michael, 36–37, 39
Lewis, Evelyn, 41
liberals, 41, 76, 120, 126
Lincoln, Abraham, 159
*Los Angeles Times*, 40
*Loving v. Virginia*, 11

Marshall, Thurgood, 31
media, 40, 44, 122, 135
miscegenation, 11
Model Penal Code, 91, 93–94
morality, 29–33, 36, 56, 58–59, 79,
    99, 103–104, 108, 154, 156
Morrison, Toni, 81
Murder Victims' Families for Recon-
    ciliation, 102–103
Murray, Charles, 13

NAACP, 141
Nazis, 29, 34
Negrophobe. *See* Negrophobia
Negrophobia, 4, 17, 62–68, 73,
    75–78, 80
Nelson, Stephen, 107
New York State Crime Study 1996,
    42
noninstrumentalist, 27, 64, 77–80
North, Oliver, 24
Nugent, Paul, 118

*O'Brien v. Cunard S.S. Co.*, 85–89

ordinary man/person, 22, 57, 64,
    82–83, 85, 130

*Palmore v. Sidoti*, 69–71
*People v. Goetz*, 4, 145
Pettigrew, Thomas, 122
*Pittsburgh Post-Gazette*, 15
post-modernism, 30
post-traumatic stress disorder, 17,
    62–64, 67, 77, 82. *See also*
    Negrophobia
Powell, Laurence M., 5
prejudice, 11–12, 17, 32, 59–60,
    63–64, 70, 72–73, 115, 117–127,
    129, 133, 135–144, 146, 149–153,
    158
Procrustean bed. *See* Procrustes
Procrustes, 25, 28, 84, 157
prostitutes, 47, 49, 52
provocation doctrine, 92–93
psychoanalytic theory, 128
*Pulp Fiction*, 29–30
pure-merit paradigm, 107

race, 3–5, 29, 34, 41, 47, 51, 53,
    55–57, 61, 67, 68–70, 77, 82, 88,
    115–116, 132–133, 138, 142,
    148–150; caste system, 11; con-
    sciousness, 6–7, 118, 133, 158;
    favoritism, 59, 72, 76–78, 80,
    120, 125, 128, 146, 152
racial bias. *See* discrimination; race,
    favoritism
racial discrimination. *See* discrimina-
    tion
racial fear, 4–5, 20–21, 39, 45, 66,
    146
racism, 12–13, 17, 19, 35, 40, 43, 58,
    60, 119, 126–128
racist, 16, 19–22, 27, 30, 32, 34, 36,
    43, 57–58, 61, 68–69, 79, 100,
    118, 119, 127, 157

rape, 53–54, 61, 73
Rawlsian veil of ignorance, 104
realists, 89
reasonable man/person. *See* ordinary man/person
reasonableness, 3–5, 8, 21, 25–26, 33, 39, 47–50, 55, 59, 63, 65, 71, 81, 92, 94, 143, 156–157; objective test, 26, 83–84; standard, 22, 25, 32–34, 56, 79, 82; subjective test, 26, 49, 62
Reasonable Racist. *See* racist
redlining, 14
reverse discrimination. *See* discrimination
Royko, Mike, 43

scapegoating, 81, 112
self-defense, 3–5, 21, 23, 51, 59–60, 78, 82–83, 90, 145
Sherry, Suzanna, 53–54
shopkeepers, 23–24, 35, 45, 56
Simpson, O. J., 7
slavery, 11, 29, 30, 157
slaves. *See* slavery
Slotnick, Barry, 5, 146, 148
socially marginalized groups, 6–7, 17, 101, 105–106, 109, 114, 121
Stanford, 154–155
statistically deviant, 19, 27, 103
statistical probabilities, 3
statistics, 12, 16, 36–37, 39–41, 45–46, 51, 55, 57, 72
Steele, Claude, 154–155
stereotype-congruent responses, 122–126, 136, 139–140, 144–145, 150–151
stereotypes, 3, 5, 12–13, 17, 19, 36, 40, 41, 71–73, 75–76, 79, 100, 115, 117–122, 124–125, 129–130,

132–141, 143–151, 153–155, 158–159
storekeepers. *See* shopkeepers
studies, 59, 119, 123, 152, 157; FBI Uniform Crime Reports, 40; 1990 University of Chicago, 20; 1996 New York State Study on Sentencing, 42
Sweet, Ossian Henry, 141, 143–144, 153

Tasmanian devil, 5, 149
Ten Commandments, 30
*T. J. Hooper*, 33
Tomlinson, Judge John G., Jr., 63–64
Travolta, John, 29

unemployment. *See* discrimination, employment
University of California at Los Angeles, 110
University of Virginia, 28
*U.S. News & World Report*, 35, 44

value judgments, 8
violence, 2

*Wall Street Journal*, 108
War on Drugs, 37
*Washington Post*, 35, 64
Wasik, Martin, 93
Williams, Patricia, 146
Williams, Walter, 36
Winfrey, Oprah, 3
witches, 23, 25
Wonder, Stevie, 3

Yale Law School, 43
Young, Charles, 110